MONARCH OF THE WESTERN SKIES

The Story of a Wedge-tailed Eagle

BY

C.K. THOMPSON

Author of "King of the Ranges," Etc.

This edition published 2017
By Living Book Press
147 Durren Rd, Jilliby, 2259
Copyright © The Estate of C.K. Thompson, 1946

The publisher would like to give a huge 'Thank You' to the author's family
for their assistance in making this book available once more.

National Library of Australia Cataloguing-in-Publication entry:

Creator:	Thompson, C.K. (Charles Kenneth), 1904-1980 author
Title:	Old Bob's birds / C.K. Thompson
ISBN:	9780648104810 (paperback)
Target Audience:	For primage school age.
Subjects:	Adventure stories, Australian.
	Wedge-tailed eagle--Australia--Juvenile fiction.
	Australia--Juvenile fiction.

MONARCH OF THE WESTERN SKIES

DEDICATION

To
THELMA
With Love and Appreciation

FOREWORD
WILL LAWSON
(Famous Australian balladist, poet and author.)

This story of the great wedge-tailed eagle of Australia—the second largest eagle in the world—is one to thrill the imagination and enlighten the minds of young and old alike.

Mr. Thompson evidently has studied his subject closely, both by patient watching and determined mountain climbing, to come, one would judge, almost to the eagle's eyrie!

Already well known to adult readers in another realm of our literature, he made an instant appeal to book lovers with that splendid nature story, "King of the Ranges," intended primarily for younger minds.

He has now done for the wedge-tail eagle what he did for the kangaroo; and it is noteworthy that in this story, as in "King of the Ranges," he does not spoil his narrative by making his bird and animal characters talk. To have done so would have created that air of unreality which is so apparent in "humanised" nature stories. Mr. Thompson writes of birds and animals—for there are many more than the great eagle in "Monarch of the Western Skies"—as Nature created them. He writes of them sympathetically, as one who knows them as friends; and all bird and animal watchers must become friends of the wild creatures after long association with a realm of which the busy world takes little cognisance.

The creatures of bush, river, plain and air, are Australia's greatest heritage of nationality. They are just as important as are we Australians ourselves; and the more we know about them, the better Australians we shall be; and the less will we be inclined to shoot or otherwise destroy them indiscriminately.

From an entertainment aspect, the author has done a good job; from the educational viewpoint, an even better one.

And with the great Wedge-tail soaring high as the crowning glory of Nature's ruthless, yet beautiful world, we may vision the great plains and mountains, rivers and bushlands, which are the setting for this very fine story.

WILL LAWSON.

CONTENTS

CHAPTER I.

THE DESERT EYRIE

OUT on the fringe of the vast western plains a pair of wedge-tailed eagles had built their eyrie high in the branches of a massive desert oak. It was over thirty feet above the ground, a large structure of sticks lined with leaves, which had braved the desert winds and dust storms for many years.

During those years, the two eagles had seen the swimming gold of the sun at dawn; had watched with unappreciative eyes the rich red sunset painting the sandhills and frowning, rocky mountain peaks and gullies in ever-changing colours of breath-taking beauty. They had seen dream creeks and waterholes fading into elusive mirages; and, at night, when disturbed in their sleep, their dreamy eyes had chanced to note and dwell upon the millions of silver desert stars suspended in space like glittering diamonds against a background of the richest and costliest velvet.

But these fierce and fascinating beauties of a fierce and fascinating land meant nothing to the eagles. The only beauty their majestic hearts appreciated was the beauty of the hunt and the glory of the kill. This land provided them with food and with drink, and that satisfied their physical and spiritual needs. The big birds knew where to find their natural prey, how to hunt down the rabbit, the wallaby, the young kangaroo and the lizard, and, generally, they lived well. When the breeding season was over, and their young ones were ready to face the world with their own beaks and talons, the parent birds ranged far and wide, hunting, ever hunting. Hundreds, perhaps thousands of miles they might cover ere the breeding season instinctively lured them back to their favourite desert country and their ancient eyrie.

Many families had been raised and launched into the world by these two old eagles. Sometimes the seasons were bountiful and the birds lived well; sometimes drought made game scarce and life was hard for them. The present season, however, had been a good one. That arid country upon which rain might not fall for years, had been favoured by the Rain God, who had transformed it into a pleasant land on which to prey. Apart from the ever-present rabbit, the two eagles had found good hunting among the cockatoos, the galahs and other birds, and as they cleaned out their eyrie in preparation for their latest family, they were as happy and contented as savage birds of their kind were ever likely to be.

They were proud and haughty birds. Each could boast a wing-span of over seven feet, and there was nothing on the earth or in the sky of which either was afraid. Of man they had very little knowledge. Sometimes from the rare heights of the sky they had observed those curious two-legged creatures, but not often. This was not the country frequented by the human race; except a few wandering blackfellows on a walkabout to favourite yam patches or secret desert waterholes.

The Australian wedge-tail is the second largest eagle in the world. It is exceeded only by that magnificent bird which is found in the Philippine Islands and which lives on monkeys. Perhaps, unconsciously, the two old eagles realised this; certainly their dignity when in the air tended to prove that they knew they were no common birds.

Having cleaned and relined their eyrie, the wedge-tails set about the serious business of family life. Presently, two large mottled eggs occupied the nest, and in course of time produced two fluffy young eaglets.

The old birds were most attentive to their children, and many were the tit-bits brought to the eyrie to tempt their lusty appetites. Food was plentiful and the eaglets thrived mightily.

They were brothers, but not very friendly brothers. Wedge-tail, the larger of the twain, showed from the outset that he would not be content with second place; and had not his parents seen to it that the fruits of the hunt were distributed evenly between the youngsters, the smaller bird often would have gone hungry.

Wedge-tail was an aggressive and over-bearing young eagle, and his table manners left much to be desired. He wanted everything. There were occasions when the parent birds, in a hurry to return to the hunt when rabbits were plentiful, would fly to the eyrie, deposit a limp rabbit on the feeding platform, and depart immediately. It was then that Wedge-tail showed his true nature. He would appropriate the carcase to himself, disregarding his brother's frantic pleas for a share of what should have been an equally-divided meal.

But Wedge-tail was no gluttonous drone content to laze away his days in the eyrie while his parents waited upon him.

As the brother eaglets grew, and grow they did, in rapid fashion, he was the first to try his young wings. With his father, he travelled, at first unsteadily, but with ever-increasing confidence, over the wide plains in search of prey, while his smaller brother was left to the tuition of their mother.

Now, before the births of the two eaglets, the old birds had been accustomed to hunt in company after the fashion of their kind, but young Wedge-tail insinuated himself into his father's good graces and ousted his mother as hunting companion. Not that the old mother minded this at all. She knew that Wedge-tail could have no better teacher than his father and she was quite content to impart to her smaller son all the wisdom she had learned during her long and exciting lifetime.

And Wedge-tail learned many things during those interesting hunting days. At first his father would not permit him to join in the kill. There would be time enough for that later, when his young wings were stronger and he knew how to use them properly.

During Wedge-tail's school days his father at first preyed upon such small animals and birds as he could handle alone. Sometimes he had to be stern with his son. The eaglet had been given to understand quite definitely that his part, for a time, would consist merely of watching and learning. His role was to circle slowly above the ground and note what went on. Later he would be permitted to join in.

As time passed, so did the lessons progress. Like a child at school, Wedge-tail was taken step by step and from class to class.

There were many needful things that the old eagle taught him: how to dive from a great height, descend with terrific speed and force and pull out of his dizzy, headlong dive as he struck his prey; how to seize a small animal, such as a rabbit, and soar upwards again without touching the ground; how to swoop upon a young kangaroo, bury his talons into the animal's shoulders, and beat it to the ground with his powerful wings; how to drop unexpectedly from the clouds upon a swiftly-moving cockatoo or galah; and many other things.

In this arid land there were no rivers or creeks where they were needed for the creatures of the wild to drink their fills of life-giving water at any hour of the day. Here and there were water-holes, some large, but the majority all too small. Dotted over the plains, too, were numerous claypans, varying in size from several acres to several square feet; but, as all the wild things knew, these claypans were not to be depended upon, except for a brief period after rain.

Continuous winds in days long past had blown the sands away, leaving the heavier clay particles to form shallow depressions which held any rainwater while the thirsty country round them quickly absorbed it. Being no more than a few inches deep, the claypans were only transient water-containers, the hot sun quickly evaporating the water and then baking their surfaces to a concrete hardness.

Wedge-tail and his brother were shown all the waterholes and claypans within flying distance. They soon learned to distinguish between a claypan that held water and one that, reflecting the fierce heat of the molten sun, would render a downward swoop a sheer waste of flying time.

While it lasted, however, the water in a claypan was delicious, even though whitened with dissolved clay.

Routine journeys to one or another of the waterholes were taken early each morning by the wedge-tail family, and though invariably the selected hole teemed with small bird life, no other creature dared dispute the rights of the great eagles.

Wedge-tail remembered vividly his first visit to a waterhole. As he and the other three members of the family sailed into view, thousands of smaller birds, budgerigars, finches, grass-parrots, galahs and many other kinds, rose in clouds, protesting shrilly.

Wedge-tail had never before seen so many birds at one time. This waterhole was the only one for many miles around, and it lured to it many thousands of the smaller birds. Not possessing the strength and long range of eagles, these little creatures had to stay near the water, or perish trying to reach the next hole, many long and thirsty miles over the horizon.

As the young eagle drank, he was conscious of the wheeling thousands above him. In gigantic flocks the little green and yellow budgerigars almost blotted out the morning sun as they circled all together, swooping, turning and wheeling, wave after wave in perfect time.

The four eagles had hardly risen into the air before the myriads of their smaller brothers were again at the water's edge. Later, their thirsts quenched, they would fly off to their nearby haunts until the next day's sunrise brought them back again.

And so Wedge-tail's education proceeded under the careful tuition of his wise old parents. He learned the ways of the wild creatures as well as the ways of his own kith and kin.

The first occasion on which his father allowed him to share in a kill was a red-letter day for the eaglet. The old bird considered it judicious not to allow the youngster actually to attack the prey in conjunction with him. That would be a later lesson, in which close co-operation would be most essential.

Circling high in the blue one morning, the parent eagle saw, far below, a small kangaroo feeding. Wedge-tail also saw it, and looked to his father for guidance.

Like a falling star, the old eagle dropped from the sky and, reaching the kangaroo, sunk his claws into its back, buffeted its head with his powerful wings, and then soared off into the air again. Young Wedge-tail, close behind him, did not understand the move. He pulled out of his dive and soared back after his father, but that bird made no attempt again to attack the kangaroo, which was now hopping wildly towards a belt of distant scrub.

Greatly puzzled, Wedge-tail circled round and kept an eye on the animal. He did not know what was expected of him. He got no hint or assistance from his father, who continued to float high above him.

Indecision was driven from Wedge-tail's head by a daring

idea. Why not tackle the kangaroo on his own? His father had never before allowed him to do such a thing, but always there had to be a first time. Perhaps this was it.

The idea had no sooner taken shape in his head than he dropped down swiftly upon the fleeing animal, striking it savagely with his hooked beak and sharp talons as he had seen his father do.

This kangaroo was young, but it was large, and though Wedge-tail was an inexperienced bird, he had enough intelligence to realise that he alone could not hope to subdue it. His father's apparent disinterest, therefore, puzzled the youngster.

Clinging to the kangaroo and beating its head with his wings, he saw that he was making little impression on it. His inherent savage nature prevented him from giving up the struggle, so he hung on, hoping for the best, while the kangaroo bounded for the safety of the scrub.

Presently Wedge-tail heard the beating of wings above him. Instinct told him it was his father, but why didn't the old bird come to his assistance? He must surely have appreciated his son's predicament!

It was then that he lost his grip on the hide of the fleeing kangaroo, and tumbled to the ground. Jumping and wobbling around, his air-born dignity quite lost on solid earth and his pride not a little wounded, he glared with hard agate eyes after the kangaroo, to see his father swoop down on it and repeat the clawing and buffeting for a few seconds ere he once again soared upwards.

Swiftly Wedge-tail was in the air too, realisation flooding his intelligent brain. His father had not let him down, neither was the old eagle playing some stupid game to make him look foolish. No. It was all part of a careful plan. The kangaroo was too big for them to kill, either alone or in concerted attack, so his wise old parent had planned that each should chase it and attack it in turn until it was worn out. Then the kill would be simplified.

And so it proved. Now that Wedge-tail knew what was expected of him, he joined his father in the air and then, swooping and striking and soaring in turn, they had that kangaroo tired out and near to exhaustion long before it could reach the sanctuary of the distant scrub.

The kill came swiftly. With the unfortunate animal hardly able to drag one leg after another, both birds, old and young, attacked together, ripping and tearing with beaks and talons until they had deprived the kangaroo of its life.

Wedge-tail really enjoyed that meal. It was his first large prey. In after years he was to do greater deeds than this; but the deep thrill of that first great moment in his career never entirely left him.

Their feast concluded, they rose majestically, the old bird in the lead, and sailed off slowly and with dignity towards their distant lookout, leaving the remains of the kangaroo to those dark scavengers of bush, plains and desert, the crows. A flock of these had been assembling from far and near since the attack on the kangaroo had begun, and their karking voices had sounded a harsh requiem for the slaughtered marsupial.

It was now very close to the time when Wedge-tail and his brother would have to leave the parent eyrie to fend for themselves.

And so it happened that one bright morning as the four birds were perched in a large bloodwood tree, the old eagles, without the slightest hint to their sons, soared away into the heavens. Wedge-tail and his brother looked at each other with surprise and then Wedge-tail took off. With his brother close behind him, he flew swiftly after his parents, who were now dots against the white morning clouds.

But the old birds were not travelling fast and the youngsters caught up with them.

Then a most disconcerting thing occurred for, without any hint of their intentions, the parents turned on their sons, the old male selecting Wedge-tail and the female the smaller brother.

Surprised and hurt by the sudden attack of his father, Wedge-tail dropped several yards towards earth, recovered his poise, and was climbing again when he saw his father, a wheeling, menacing figure, circling above him, wings out-stretched and wedge-tail stark against the sky. At the same time he noticed, out of the corner of an eye, his small brother fleeing southwards, their mother in full chase.

His uncertainty as to what he should do quickly changed into consternation as his father swooped at him and attempted to claw his head. Wedge-tail dodged and fled. There was nothing else to do. He did not stop and he did not look behind, until he was back among the branches of the bloodwood tree. Here he discovered his woebegone brother disconsolately sitting on a branch and looking ruffled. Wedge-tail noticed that he had lost several breast feathers. Mother, apparently, had been rough and unkind to small brother!

Far away in the western sky, the two youngsters saw their parents—two fast-vanishing specks which soon disappeared altogether.

The breeding season had come round again and they were returning to their old eyrie on the fringe of the desert. Wedge-tail and his brother were not wanted any longer. Their education had been completed and the world was theirs to make the best they could of it.

Wedge-tail and his brother realised that from now on it was to be each bird for himself.

CHAPTER II.

AN EAGLE PASSES ON

AS the sun climbed higher into the heavens, hunger urged Wedge-tail to cease pining for his lost parents and to devote himself to the all-important task of earning his breakfast. As the morning meal was most unlikely to come to him, he must go in search of it.

Hitherto, he had never hunted alone, but there was nothing else to do this morning, because his brother as a partner of the chase was an unknown and untried quantity.

Leaving the bloodwood tree, he rose majestically into the air. High he climbed and still higher, before making towards a distant patch of lightly-timbered country over which, under his father's leadership, he had hunted on many occasions. Reaching the desired area, he began the usual wide circle, his eyes keenly alert for the slightest movement on the earth below. The only moving thing he saw, however, was his own shadow, but as he watched he saw a similar shadow.

Removing his gaze from the sun-warmed ground, his keen eyes raked the surrounding air. There, not far away, flew his brother, also describing the preying circle.

Instinctively the two eagles became one concentrated hunting machine. Each maintaining his own wide sweep and gradually covering a wider stretch of country, not one square foot of ground remained unexplored.

It was Wedge-tail who first saw a victim. Far below lay a small group of ironwood trees and in the shade cast by their small and narrow leaves, his quick eye had detected movement. He knew what caused it—a rabbit, or rabbits, lying in the shade to escape the heat of the sun.

There was no need here for his brother's assistance! Swiftly he dropped and as he did so, he noticed that there were four or five rabbits in the group. So much the better for both birds. If his brother was as alert as he, breakfast for each was there for the taking.

That Brother was equally alert was quickly demonstrated for, as soon as he saw Wedge-tail fall, he, too, threw himself into the downward plunge, planing speedily towards the shade of the ironwoods. The rabbits were taken completely by surprise. One moment there were five of them. Suddenly the sky became overcast. There was a flurry of giant wings and three terror-stricken bunnies gazed with horror at their feathered visitors who towered over them with fierce eyes and menacing beaks. The other two rabbits took no interest in the proceedings. Lifeless they lay, flattened under the talons of Wedge-tail and his brother.

But the eagles were not interested in the terrified trio, and scarcely noticed them as, freed from the hypnotic spell cast on them by the birds' arrival, they fled into the open and down their burrows like three furry bullets.

Their meal over, Wedge-tail and his brother ascended

into the upper air and proceeded slowly eastwards. The rabbits had not been large ones and it was not long ere each bird again felt the urge to eat.

A flight of several miles brought them into country that was unfamiliar to them. They had left the desert fringe and had passed over the low rocky range. Here the earth was not so bare, and as they floated easily along, Wedge-tail noted several moving objects. He could not determine what they were, so planed down to obtain a closer view.

It was his first encounter with sheep and the first thought that entered his feathered head was, were they good to eat? Their size, he saw, precluded a lone attack. Would his brother and he, in combined adventure, be able to cope with one of them?

Before doing anything rash, however, he deemed it wise to investigate these strange animals at close quarters.

Dropping earthwards, not in the hunting dive, but in a slow and cautious circle, Wedge-tail alighted within a few yards of half a dozen sheep. Tensely cautious, and ready to spring into the air if they should attack him, he studied them closely. They were fully grown and, at close quarters, looked much too large for him to tackle.

Brother had not followed Wedge-tail to the ground when he had seen he was not on a killing hunt, but circled uncertainly a hundred feet up, watching and waiting.

On the ground, Wedge-tail was a far different bird from the noble creature of the air. His big wings and thick feathered legs made his movements clumsy. If he were slow in his movements he could walk with some dignity, but any tendency to hurry turned him into a hopping, flopping ridiculous bird.

Standing like a grave statue, he could not make up his mind what to do, and was on the point of joining his brother in the heavens when Brother, impatient to learn what was going on, planed down and joined him on the ground.

Brother was hungry, and was minded to try conclusions with a sheep· without counting the consequences, but he received no encouragement from the cautious Wedge-tail. As for the sheep, they regarded the two birds with some concern. They had seen their kind before and associated unpleasant things with them.

None of the sheep were over-burdened with brains, and as long as the eagles made no attempt to interfere with them, the woolly animals were content not to initiate any moves. Not for a single moment would any of them have considered attacking these visitors from the clouds. Being sheep, they were not built that way. But one or two of them did vaguely associate these eagles with something unpleasant, though they did not know what caused the mistrust. Deep thinking is not a characteristic of one of nature's stupidest animals. They live for to-day. Yesterday is as if it has never been, while to-morrow is something that might never be.

An old ram ceased grazing for a moment to stare at the eagles who stood like frozen statues and returned the stare. The old ram in his dim brain tried to catch some elusive thought, some intangible thread of recollection, but it was too much for him, and he resumed his grass munching with a slight headache.

The elusive something that had escaped the animal was that just after he had been born, a wedge-tail eagle had tried to carry him off, but had been detected in the act and scared away by a human boundary rider. Such an experience would have scarred deeply the memory of an intelligent human or beast, but that old sheep was not distinguished for its sensitive reasoning powers.

Deeming it profitless to remain there longer, Wedge-tail took off. Before leaving the vicinity he wheeled slowly over the paddock, taking stock of the countryside. Then he noticed that his brother was not with him. A glance earthwards revealed him still on the ground.

As Wedge-tail watched, he saw his brother jumping and wobbling over the stubbled earth towards what looked like a rabbit. In an instant Wedge-tail was planing swift! y back to the ground. If there was any food about he intended to share it-or appropriate the whole lot if possible.

He reached his brother to find him standing over a dead rabbit. Wedge-tail had never before eaten anything he had not himself killed; nevertheless. he had a keen appetite and meant to have a share of this morsel.

Brother had quite a different idea. He intended to eat the lot. As Wedge-tail jumped at him, he uttered a harsh scream and prepared to do battle for the trophy, now held firmly beneath his talons.

Wedge-tail made a vicious peck at his brother and beat his

wings threateningly. Brother pecked back just as viciously and then threw himself at Wedge-tail. Knocked temporarily off his balance and unable to recover quickly, Wedge-tail was considerably chagrined to observe his brother take to the air, the rabbit firmly held in his talons.

It was a matter of seconds before Wedge-tail, too, was on the wing, but he disdained to follow his brother, who was flying rapidly towards a tall gum tree half a mile away. Here, perched safely on a big branch, he proceeded to lunch off the dead bunny, scattering the bones and unwanted portions on the ground below.

In the meantime, Wedge-tail was searching for any other rabbits, dead or alive, that might be around, but, except for the sheep, he could detect no life below.

He was still circling when he was joined by his brother. He made no sign, because he was not pleased with that brother.

Taking up a position about 50 feet below Wedge-tail, the other eagle began to circle also. Wedge-tail watched him with dislike, half-inclined to dive down and peck him on the neck. He was a selfish and unbrotherly bird in Wedge-tail's opinion; which showed that Wedge-tail had a memory that, if not short, was at least convenient, for, had not he, himself, in their eaglet days, been the glutton of the eyrie, ever ready to appropriate to himself the food that belonged equally to both?

As he watched his brother wheeling below, his sharp eyes noticed that something was wrong with him. No longer was he sailing in graceful circles, but was flapping his wings as if in distress. A wedge-tail eagle can sail in the sky for a long time without a single wing-beat, and Brother was quite capable of that, as Wedge-tail knew. What then, was the trouble?

Wedge-tail paused in flight as an agonised scream floated up to him and he saw his brother flap his wings in wild flight. Across the plains he went, making for the waterhole just visible in the distance. Suddenly his speed slackened and he began to lose height. Slowly at first, and then with gathering momentum, he started to drop.

Forgetting his dislike of a brother who had not shared a meal with him, Wedge-tail planed swiftly after him and so fast was he that they reached earth at exactly the same moment.

Without question, the other eagle was in sore distress. He lay on the ground with feebly-beating wings and making harsh, croaking noises which startled the grazing sheep, causing them to rush swiftly from the vicinity. Then two crows began a mournful, but anticipatory karking from a low bush, which made Wedge-tail glare with hate-filled eyes in their direction.

His brother was dying. Of that there was no question. And he was dying a pitiful death, for the rabbit he had eaten had been poisoned. At sundown the previous day, stockmen had laid poison baits for rabbits. Among the unlucky animals· that had eaten a bait was the rabbit off which Brother had lunched. Feeling the poison taking effect, an overpowering thirst had come to him and he was making a frantic effort to reach water when the poison did its deadly work and he crashed to earth.

There was nothing Wedge-tail could do about the matter, but the great eagle stood there somberly watching his brother, whose struggles were becoming fainter and fainter. No more would he range the open skies, hunting for his meals over desert, plains and bush.

Wedge-tail's brother and companion was dead. A short ten minutes earlier, that magnificent bird, filled with the joy of the hunt and so vitally alive, had been with him high in the blue. Now he was just a pathetic mound of feathers-food for the scavenger crows that waited, like impatient harbingers of doom, in the low bush nearby.

On heavy wings and with a heavy heart, Wedge-tail soared into the clouds. The crows left the low bush and hopped towards the dead eagle . . .

During the days and weeks that followed, Wedge-tail prospected many miles of country. He did not return to the desert fringe where he had been born, neither did he again visit the sheep country where he had lost his brother.

And so his life went on.

It was several seasons before he found a mate. The delay was not occasioned through any desire on his part to live alone, but merely because his species in his new area was not plentiful. Occasionally he met others of his kind, but did not co-operate with them in the hunt, mainly because they were in pairs and in the life of an eagle, as in the lives of many other species, human or animal. two is company.

Now, had Wedge-tail known the reason for this dearth of his species in this stretch of country, he might have felt some concern for his own safety.

A hungry wedge-tailed eagle had stolen a lamb from a paddock. He had been detected in the act by a stockman. The lamb had been but a small weak thing whose expectation of life in any case, was not bright. This, however, was beside the point. It was a lamb, and an eagle had killed it. What was more, the eagle had flown off with it in its talons.

The story gained in the telling, as a lot of stories do, and so exaggerated did it become that stockmen and boundary riders, without any evidence to support their stories, were telling each other that scores of lambs were being eaten by eagles, and that something would have to be done about it. Something was done. War was waged against all eagles with poison and with rifle.

Wedge-tail's brother had been unfortunate in eating the poisoned rabbit, because it had not been left there for a passing eagle. It had been killed by a bait deliberately left for rabbits.

In blissful ignorance of these sinister occurrences which had so reduced the number of eagles in this part of the country, Wedge-tail lived serenely on, hunting and killing his meals as he had done since he had made his first kill under the critically-watchful eyes of his veteran father.

And kill his meals he did always. He never stooped to eating dead things. Something deep down inside him warned him against that practice. Perhaps it was the recollection of what had happened to his brother; perhaps it was because he thrilled too much to the excitement of the hunt to descend to the questionable habit of eating carrion like a common crow.

Wedge-tail did not like crows. He regarded them as so many parasites that hung around an eagle after he had caught his dinner, hoping to collect the scraps, and so win a meal without having to work for it. There actually had been occasions when, lunching off a young kangaroo or wallaby, or perhaps a large lizard, he had had to chase away impudent crows which had attempted to sneak portions from under his very beak. One of these fine days, Wedge-tail told himself savagely, he would attack some of these wretched birds and teach the survivors such a lesson that they would be glad to hunt their own meals and leave a hardworking and conscientious eagle in peace.

Most of the crows in those parts had a healthy respect for Wedge-tail, but there were other hardened villains who had not.

Floating high above a patch of mulga, Wedge-tail noticed a small flock of galahs leave it and fly, screaming loudly, towards another group of trees, about a mile away. He had not tasted galah for some time.

Like an arrow from a powerful bow, down he went travelling with such speed that the galahs did not see him until he was among them.

Selecting one plump bird, with accuracy timed to the

fraction of a second he soon had it tightly gripped in his talons, his whirling wings knocking its companions right and left. A small cloud of feathers floated away on the faint breeze as Wedge-tail gained height again.

The galah, however, was not quite dead, and with one last effort managed to give Wedge-tail a sharp nip on the toe. Surprised, the eagle loosened his grip and like a ball of tattered feathers, the galah went tumbling downwards. Quite unperturbed, Wedge-tail poised himself for an instant, and then dropped like a bullet. He had that galah firmly in his talons long before it reached the earth, and went off to finish his meal in the peaceful foliage of a big stringy-bark tree.

CHAPTER III

WEDGE-TAIL FINDS A MATE

THE young red kangaroo, lying at his ease among the salt-bush in the early morning sunshine, was at peace with the world. What brain he possessed was quite inactive. He was not even thinking of food, which was unlike him.

Dreamily he scratched his head and then his stomach, yawned mightily and rolled over on his side. Several inquisitive flies tried to climb into his right eye and he brushed them away with a lazy paw.

With his eyes half-closed he was dropping into a gentle doze when something hit the saltbush above his head and dropped gently on to his stomach. Swinging his head round he saw that it was a small stick. For some seconds he lay still, but nothing else happened. All around him the scrub was quiet, except for the chirping of small birds. A lizard scampered over the sand near him and he heard a crow's melancholy cawing in the distance.

Everything appeared to be in order and in any event a small stick could not harm him. He sighed, screwed up his eyes, twitched his ears, wrinkled his nose and prepared to doze again. He lay there among the saltbush half-asleep for about five minutes before anything happened again, and this time he had the wits almost scared out of his red hide as a very large stick whistled from the air and struck him fair and square on the top of the head.

Leaping to his legs he pawed at his head and glared wildly around him. He saw nothing, but on the ground at his feet was a big stick. As he looked down at it a black and menacing shadow passed over it. That was something tangible. He had no need to risk dislocating his neck to learn what owned that shadow. It belonged to a Wedge-tailed eagle.

The red kangaroo had had some experience of eagles. Though it had not happened to him personally, his fellow kangaroos had been attacked by these birds. It was only a few weeks previously that two of them had trapped a playmate of his as they both fed in a small rocky gorge. What they had done to that playmate the red kangaroo did not know, because he had not stayed there to make notes of the startling occurrence.

Cowering under the protecting saltbush, he was undecided what to do. The eagle might not be interested in him, but he was uneasy and was taking no chances. He did not realise that the bird, a husky young female, had dropped the sticks on him to scare him into the open where he would be an easy prey. He knew nothing about the habits of these eagles, neither did he thirst after knowledge. All he wanted was to be left alone.

Though nothing further happened to perturb him, he was not happy now under the saltbush. He wanted to leave, but feared to. He twitched his ears in indecision and then, hopping into the open, stared around him uneasily, his ears alert to catch any sound that might warn him if he were in danger. The finches were still chirping among the bushes, and the crows were still karking in the distance.

The kangaroo paused, sat back, and listened intently. Then he hopped a few yards, only to stop again and glance back anxious! y towards the saltbush that had been sheltering him. There was nothing he could see to cause him the slightest unease. He toyed with the idea of returning and then became aware of something biting his chest. With busy paw he scratched the offending spot and sat up straight again to listen.

He was becoming less alert. His dull brain had almost forgotten the sticks and the menacing shadow. Nothing had happened for quite five minutes, so nothing was likely to happen now.

So thought the foolish kangaroo as he began leisurely to hop away. Far above him, the Wedge-tailed eagle, hardly moving, careful now that her shadow did not disturb the marsupial below, appreciated every movement it made. The bird was waiting patiently until the kangaroo got so far. away from the saltbush that he could not return to it when she launched her attack. While he had been under the bush she had been unable to attack him, so had adopted a trick often employed by the eagles to scare game into the open.

Quite satisfied now that his fears had been groundless, the red kangaroo hopped leisurely towards another clump of bushes about a quarter of a mile away, while fierce agate eyes behind a hooked beak watched him intently.

The moment for the attack had arrived and the eagle was about to go into her power-dive when she sensed the presence of another bird. Circling near her was a magnificent male: Wedge-tail.

With an anxious glance towards the red kangaroo, she made an upward swoop to get above Wedge-tail, but that experienced warrior was too alert for that. As she swept upwards, so did he, and in the resultant flurry, they almost collided. Angrily drawing away, the female eagle gave a harsh scream which indicated to Wedge-tail that he was not wanted. Abashed, he ascended slowly into the clouds.

A sharp gaze earthwards showed the female eagle that the red kangaroo had almost reached the protecting saltbush. There was no time to lose.

With wings half-folded, she plummeted down, to land on the kangaroo's shoulders just as he reached the saltbush. Sinking her talons into his hide and hooking her beak into his neck, she gave a prodigious backward heave and literally dragged him into the open. That was all right as far as it went, but she quickly found she had taken on a little more than she could handle. From her vantage point in the sky she had seen the kangaroo enter the first patch of bushes but had been unable to judge his size. Flying off to the nearest tree, she had torn a small twig from it and had dropped this on the saltbush to scare the 'roo into the open. The scheme had failed, so she had returned to the tree for a large stick.

This time the ruse was successful. but still it had not given her any idea as to the size of the prey.

She was only a young eagle and it was her first attempt at the lone hunting of large prey. Like Wedge-tail in his early days she had learned her hunting lore from her parents who, when the time was ripe, had cast her into the world to fend for herself.

But this was no time for reminiscing. She had a large young kangaroo on her talons and hardly knew what to do with it now that she had it.

Clawing the animal's hide and beating at him with her big wings, she tried to tear his back with her hooked beak, but the kangaroo was not just standing there placidly allowing her to do it. Desperately he tried to reach the bushes in the hope that he would be able to brush her off; and as desperately she endeavoured to prevent it.

It was then that she received the assistance· she urgently needed. Up in the blue, Wedge-tail saw and appreciated the struggle, but until now had not felt called upon to interfere. In his first brief encounter with the lady, she had shown him plainly that she did not desire his company. That being so, he had enough wit and intelligence to realise that any hunt in her company would be lacking in that co-operation so essential to a successful killing. Failure would follow any enterprise in which the two birds did not act as one.

He could see, however, that the lady would never get that kangaroo if she had to depend wholly on her own prowess. The red 'roo had now thrown himself to the ground, dislodging his feathered foe, and in another few seconds he would be among those bushes from under which it would take more than one eagle to drag him.

Those few vitally-needed seconds, however) were not allowed him for, ere he could drag himself forward one more foot, Wedge-tail had screamed into the fray.

Together the two great birds assailed the unfortunate animal, ripping and tearing with beaks and with talons like steel rakes. Disregarding his frantic struggles, his thrashing tail and weaving front paws, they pulled him into the open and literally tore him apart. Their enmity of a few minutes before was quite forgotten. Side by side they feasted royally on tender kangaroo steaks, and when they could eat no more, rose heavily and languidly, side by side. Reaching a large tree, they settled on a branch and prepared to indulge in a long loaf.

Thus it came about that Wedge-tail met and won his first mate.

Day by day and week by week the two eagles lived and hunted together, spending their days in the air above the plains, the hills and the bush, and their nights in the most convenient tree. It was a carefree, happy existence, and each bird was wholly content in the company of the other.

The breeding season found them in the rather mountainous country on the fringe of the plains and there they built their first eyrie, selecting a large tree over 80 feet in height. They ranged far and wide for the huge sticks to build the eyrie, and when they found themselves at a long distance from home with sticks too heavy to transport in their talons, they left them there and obtained the necessary large ones from the eyrie tree itself.

Selecting a large dead limb, Wedge-tail or his mate would jump on it until it broke under his or her weight. If it was above the nest, it was guided down to it and then dragged into position. If, however, the desired stick was below the eyrie, the big bird, after breaking it off, would swoop down, catch it and literally push it, pendulum fashion, to the nest.

And in those joyous nest-building days, Wedge-tail and his mate were not above a little frivolity in their happiness. Sometimes, as one or the other was flying home with a stick, he or she would drop it and then quickly swoop and catch it again. At times Wedge-tail would fly high above his mate and drop the stick for her to catch. Then the procedure would be reversed.

During the seasons that followed, they raised and trained several broods of young eaglets. On one occasion an egg vanished from the eyrie. Wedge-tail suspected a thieving crow. The only evidence he had to support this charge was the fact that he had seen a crow in the tree shortly after the egg had disappeared.

Wedge-tail, as we have recorded already, did not like crows. These black birds with white eyes and that melancholy harsh karking that seemed to intensify the loneliness of the plains rather than relieve it, were his special dislike. They were wary birds, these crows, combining intelligence with instinctive cunning, and so were very hard to catch.

Not that Wedge-tail had ever tried to catch any; but he had promised himself often that if he ever got close enough to a crow to inflict damage on it, he would do so with the greatest alacrity and pleasure.

Crows stooped to low tricks apart from stealing the eggs of other birds. They were known to pick the eyes out of sick sheep and lambs. Such a low-down habit did not specially disgust Wedge-tail, some of whose own habits were not above criticism; but the injustice of the thing lay in the fact that sheep owners seemed to tolerate the ebony devils while waging bitter war on the eagles whose only crime was the theft of an occasional lamb.

Of course, there was nothing to prevent Wedge-tail seeking out the nests of the crows and doing a little bit of despoiling of his own-except his majestic pride. He had seen many crows' nests in the high trees. They were built like his own eyrie and contained dull green eggs blotched and spotted with brown.

Another bird that annoyed him, for a different reason, was the magpie. On many occasions pairs of these bold black and white songsters had actually assaulted him, chasing him through the air and pecking him viciously. That generally occurred if he chanced to be in the neighbourhood of their nests. They were pests, but he could understand and appreciate their urge to protect their homes-not that he would ever have despoiled one. He had no desire to attack a magpie. That bird was a gentleman compared with a crow.

Fierce bird that he was, arrogant and intolerant where

his own rights were concerned, Wedge-tail did not in the least mind when a couple of tiny yellow-tailed thornbills attached their pretty little nests to the bottom of his eyrie. He knew that they did this, as several species of small tom-tits do, to escape the attention of prowling butcherbirds and other predatory slayers.

Resting in his look-out post-a huge limb at the side of the eyrie. Wedge-tail often deigned to notice the little birds. He regarded them with benevolent condescension as they gathered the materials to build their two-storey nest-a domed structure with an open nest on top, and a cunningly-contrived side entrance, to trick cuckoos in search of a convenient home in which to lay their eggs.

These little birds would never steal his eggs, Wedge-tail knew. The magpies had their own eggs to guard. So it must have been the crows. Well, they would suffer for it some day.

The two eagles used their eyrie in the large tree for several seasons and were then forced to build another. They had been hundreds of miles away one year, and, therefore, had not the slightest inkling that anything had gone wrong until, the breeding urge upon them, they had returned to the tree to find it on the ground and the eyrie smashed and wrecked. A storm had blown down the old tree, and the eagles were homeless.

Not caring to remain in that vicinity, they moved west-wards. Searching for a suitable place, they found it near some rocky hills.

Being intelligent birds they decided not to erect their

new home in a tree, but to establish it where it really would have permanency.

The spot selected was ideal. It was a rocky ledge high up the side of a single peak and with it they were more than satisfied.

The new eyrie established, they set about raising their newest family and when the young birds were ready, trained them in the same fashion as a long line of their kith and kin had done before them.

And so the seasons came and went.

CHAPTER IV

THE STEALER OF EGGS

EXCEPT for one high peak, that reared its summit skywards like the upraised finger of a reclining giant, the mountain spur was nothing more than a straightened necklace of rocky hills. Unlike the Great Dividing Range of the east, where towering peaks kiss the clouds and shady gullies with cool liquid pools and graceful ferns beckon invitingly to the bush lover, this western range was hard and unpicturesque.

The proud and majestic wedge-tailed eagle, brooding in his lookout post—a high tree that jutted from the side of the lone peak—had no interest in scenery, grand or desolate.

Thirty feet beneath him was his eyrie, a great mass of varied material, mostly sticks, the accumulation of years. It was built on a ledge of rock that protruded several feet from the side of the peak and about fifteen feet from its summit.

Wedge-tail gazed down at the eyrie with savage agate eyes, his whole being, from his dark brown plumage to his wickedly hooked beak, permeated with cold fury. At the moment the eyrie was empty, except for one large egg. His beloved mate, feeling in need of exercise after a long period of brooding on the nest, was away hunting for her morning meal. A rabbit perhaps, a small wallaby maybe—yes, and even a young lamb.

That was in the natural order of things. It was not with his mate that Wedge-tail was angry. Something of major importance had upset the great bird to such an extent that, instead of accompanying his mate on her search for food, he was perched on his lookout limb like the very statue of doom itself.

Sweeping the sun-warmed plains beneath with eyes as keen as any microscope and seeing nothing to interest him, he glared at the sky. Far up and to the west, he noted several specks, like minute ink spots on an azure vase. One of them might be his mate and it might not. Wedge-tail was not interested in his mate just then.

Fluffing out his feathers and then settling down again, he dropped his gaze to the eyrie. When his yes noted that single egg, they blazed; and the blaze was not one of pride of achievement.

On the previous morning at this very hour, there had been two eggs in that eyrie. Now there was only one, and it was that fact that filled Wedge-tail with cold fury.

He had little doubt that a detestable crow was the culprit, but was not wholly convinced of that. Some prowling creature had taken the egg while he and his mate had been away seeking their breakfasts. It was a loss, and an insult, that the eagle would not tolerate. What manner of impudent creature was this that had desecrated the regal home of the mighty monarch of the western skies?

Passionately, Wedge-tail desired to know, and he intended to find out. He had lost an egg on a previous occasion and though he suspected a crow, he meant now to establish the identity of the thief once and for all.

Wise in the ways of the wild and of nature's fellow-creatures in the great Australian outback, he felt certain that the culprit would return. This time there would be no empty nest awaiting the easy tooth or claw of the despoiler. Wedge-tail was resolved to catch the thief if he had to sit up there all day and all night.

It would not be correct to say that Wedge-tail was a conceited bird. His majestic dignity lay upon him unconsciously as a birthright. But he was fully aware of his great prowess in battle and in the hunt, and was equally conscious of the fact that his species was the greatest flying bird in Australia. He knew, too, from experience, that he and his kind ruled the skies and most of the animal kingdom beneath.

And, knowing all this, Wedge-tail felt the loss of that egg very keenly. He knew exactly what he intended to do to the creature that had stolen it—if he could get his beak and claws into it. Not for a moment did he weigh the possible results of the encounter. Though he did not know what he was likely to meet, neither did he care a jot, nor count the possible cost.

Wedge-tail was a bird of the highest courage. There was not one ounce of fear in the whole of his great body; neither was there much sweetness or benevolence.

Suddenly he stiffened into immobility, his unwinking eyes fixed on a piece of rock that stuck out from the mountainside some feet below the ledge which bore his eyrie. He had seen a movement—just a faint flurry of something indeterminate, but certainly a movement.

The next half-minute passed without incident, and then he saw a snake-like head appear around a small corner. It was followed, very cautiously, by a pair of claws and then a chest. Wedge-tail, his agate eyes glued to the spot, saw that it was the front-quarters of a large goanna.

The ledge that the goanna was negotiating in its laborious, upward climb, was about 35 feet from where the vengeful eagle watched, a distance too short for him to swoop with that great speed he knew so well how to employ.

Wedge-tail recognised that he must amend this. He had perched on his lookout to watch for whatever had desecrated his eyrie, knowing that had he been aloft and circling, probably he would have been seen from the ground and the unknown visitor would not have paid the return visit for the other egg.

As he watched, he saw the goanna claw his way up a foot or so and then sneak into a cleft in the rock, from which his tail depended. Presently the reptile disappeared altogether and at that moment the eagle launched himself on silent wings—not at the disappearing goanna, but upwards in a swift ascent.

He had to risk the goanna seeing him, but that reptile was having enough trouble negotiating the rocky side of the cliff without star-gazing. Just below the eyrie were some small tufts of grass and these gave him enough foothold to haul himself aloft after he had crawled up the small fissure into which Wedge-tail had seen him vanish.

His wicked head was just over the edge of the eyrie ledge when Wedge-tail struck. From the sky he screamed and, with talons outstretched, tore the goanna from the cliff face. Rising swiftly to just above the top of the lookout tree, Wedge-tail released his hold. The goanna went hurtling to earth, to strike the rocks hundreds of feet below.

Screaming with vindictive triumph, Wedge-tail whirled aloft, hung in mid-air, with never a wingflap, for several seconds, and then volplaned to earth, alighting within a few feet of the slowly writhing goanna.

Leaning forward, he seized it in his powerful beak, shook it a few times and then cast it from him. For a few seconds he watched his dying enemy, and then, without disdaining to convert it into a meal, rose from the ground at a low angle and slowly soared into the blue. Quite satisfied that the menace to his remaining egg had been disposed of for good, he did not return to his lookout, but sailed rapidly in the direction his mate had taken some time earlier.

It was high over the lightly-timbered country that he found her. Evidently she had not found the hunting good, for she was circling widely, keen eyes fixed on the ground. Ascending many feet above her, Wedge-tail started to circle also. There was no need for either bird to compare notes or plan out the method of the hunt. Their strategy was instinctive, born of a long line of predatory eagles.

In addition to this ingrained characteristic, Wedge-tail and his mate, through years of intimate association, were perfect hunting partners. They knew and anticipated each other's moves. Not every eagle keeps a partner for life. Some flighty birds tire of each other after one or two seasons, while others are content with their first choice, and keep together for years.

So it was with Wedge-tail and his noble mate. She was a bird not so darkly-coloured as he, and with not such a wide span of wing; but as a huntress she had no peer in his eyes. He could always depend upon her for intelligent co-operation, and she upon him.

When Wedge-tail, soaring on unmoving wings above his mate, saw her descend at terrific speed, he immediately plunged down after her. He had not seen their intended prey. He had no knowledge what they were to attack. It might be a wallaby, a young kangaroo, a dingo, or just a scared rabbit or two. She might need his help and she might not. No matter what the position was, he was there ready.

As the ground rushed rapidly to meet him, Wedge-tail saw the victim. It was a wallaby which, becoming urgently aware of the menace from the skies, was hopping frantically towards some rocks between which he hoped to slip for sanctuary.

His mate flew at that wallaby with the speed of a falling star and, like an aeroplane piloted by the hand of a master ace, pulled out of the dizzy dive as it struck the terrified animal. Wedge-tail was a split second behind her, and as she struck the wallaby on the shoulders, he, swooping low enough almost to touch the ground, struck it in the back. With her claws sunk in its shoulders, she began to beat the wallaby with her wings about the head and face, while Wedge-tail fell to work with both beak and claws.

Though he had been thrown down under the weight of the attack, the wallaby was a powerfully-built one. Terror and the overwhelming urge of self-preservation forced him back on his legs, but again he was overthrown. Refusing to give in without a passionate struggle, the wallaby flopped his tail and his front paws flailed and beat at the feathered furies. A sharp blow managed to dislodge the female eagle, and for a moment the wallaby was able to bring into play his powerful hind legs each of which was armed with a sharp claw. He was now lying on his back and as he kicked upwards, he got home a slash on Wedge-tail's breast. The sleek plumage, however, did not lend itself to easy ripping, and the blow, apart from depriving Wedge-tail of a few feathers, made him angrier.

The end was not long in coming. Two huge curved beaks and two pairs of sharp talons were weapons against which the wallaby's armory was not proof.

Wedge-tail and his matchless mate breakfasted off tasty marsupial that morning.

CHAPTER V.

THE SHEEP COUNTRY

IT had been a mild winter and on several runs on the sheep station lambing time already had commenced. For the stockmen the lambing season was always an anxious one with plenty of work to be done. The mother ewes and their small white unsteadily-footed children had to be cared for until the little lambs were able to look after themselves.

Ever since the first flush of dawn had lightened the eastern sky, two stockmen had been riding the paddocks, listening and watching and searching. Their keen eyes raked hollows and bushes, gullies and hillocks, their ears alert to catch the slightest sound that would reveal the presence of a newborn lamb and its mother.

Far to the east the mountain range was slowly shedding its night raiment of mist and cloud under the gentle persuasion of the rising sun, and though it was a sight familiar to the stockmen, its glamorous beauty never failed to enthral them.

Reining their horses to a halt, they sat idly in their saddles gazing eastwards where the sun was now raising its shining head above the top of a solitary mountain peak that thrust skywards like the up-pointed finger of a reclining giant.

"Looks like another warm fine day, Jack," Bert Summers remarked to his friend.

"Yes," Jack Howard agreed. "A few wet days would not come amiss, though."

Idly he glanced overhead. There, far above the paddock a large bird wheeled slowly, its wedge-shaped tail showing sharp and clear against the dark blue background.

"Well, I'm blessed!" he exclaimed. "Old Wedge-tail is back again! You could almost set your watch by that bird!"

"How do you know it is he?" asked Summers, his eyes following the wheeling eagle. "There are plenty of wedge-tails in this country, and I for one, would not like to bet on the identity of any particular one."

Howard smiled.

"I am not going to bet on it, Bert," he said, "but you must admit that every lambing time, old Wedge-tail is first out to survey the paddocks. One of these days I am going to take my rifle and ride over to that mountain!"

"Don't evade the question, Jack," persisted his friend. "How do you know it is old Wedge-tail?"

"Because, during the past five or six years, every time I have ridden the paddocks after young lambs I've, been spied upon by a wedge-tailed eagle. It generally happens on the first or second day out. Don't you remember last year? You were with me then and I mentioned it to you. Didn't we sit and watch him, and didn't he eventually make off towards that lone mountain? His is the only eyrie in that particular stretch of country."

"Well, well, I won't argue, old man," replied Summers with a laugh. "We'll just keep an eye on him and see if he does head for that mountain."

He paused to light his pipe. Jack Howard remained silent, gazing up at the slowly-wheeling eagle, which showed no disposition to move off towards the mountain or anywhere else.

Summers, his pipe drawing to his satisfaction, resumed his questions.

"You said a moment ago, Jack, that one of these days you would take your gun and head for that mountain. I suppose the insinuation was that you would put a bullet in Wedge-tail. Why? He might come and spy upon us at lambing time, but is that a crime meriting a bullet?"

"When an eagle steals young lambs he deserves a bullet," replied Howard.

"And does Wedge-tail do that?"

"I've never caught him at it, but all eagles steal lambs. Why should he be any different from the rest?"

"Have you ever seen any eagle take a lamb?"

"No," admitted Howard.

"Have you ever met a man who has seen an eagle take a lamb?" persisted Summers.

"Yes, I have," responded Howard. "Old Fred Bourke had one of his taken last season and actually saw the bird kill it."

"Of course, I would not be so foolish as to suggest that eagles do not kill lambs, but they more than make up for it by the number of rabbits, dingoes and foxes they destroy.

I think the whole subject of lamb-killing is grossly exaggerated," said Summers.

"The government doesn't think so," retorted his friend. "Eagles are not protected birds, you know. It is legal for anyone to kill them. I, myself, have fixed a few in my time with the gun, and also with baits."

"Baits?" questioned Summers. "I thought eagles always killed their food?"

"Don't you believe it. They eat dead things like their friends the crows. Some might not, of course, but most of them do. I've killed several by poisoning the bodies of rabbits."

"Rabbits!" exclaimed Summers passionately. "How I detest those little pests! They ruined my father. They are the greatest curse and menace in Australia. It is because eagles kill so many of them that I have a soft spot in my heart for the big birds. I would be safe in saying that for each lamb an eagle may take, he kills a thousand rabbits."

"I don't love rabbits myself. In fact I've poisoned hundreds in the course of my work. But what did you mean when you said that rabbits had ruined your father?" asked Howard.

Bert Summers did not speak for a moment. He seemed to be plunged into deep thought. Then he spoke quietly:

"My family has been mixed up with rabbits ever since they were first brought to Australia."

"Your family or the rabbits?" asked Howard with a chuckle.

His friend did not return the chuckle. The subject was a serious one with him.

"Do you know how the first rabbits came to Australia?"

he asked. "I suppose you know they are not natives of the country like emus and kangaroos, or like old Wedge-tail up there?"

"Oh, yes, I know that," said Howard. "Didn't they come out with Governor Phillip in the First Fleet?"

"I believe that about half a dozen did," said Summers. "According to books I have read, several lots were brought to Australia from Europe in the early days, mostly to be kept as pets. The real curse, however, started in Victoria in 1859."

"How do you know that?" asked the interested Howard.

"Because my old grandfather came out on the boat that brought them," said Summers grimly. "He was only a small lad at the time, but he remembered all about them and the trouble they caused. Up until the day he died he never tired of telling the story to anyone who would listen to him."

"Let's have the yarn, Bert. I'm more than interested," said Howard.

"Well, this is how grandfather used to tell the story. In 1859, a ship called 'Lightning' brought out from Europe 24 wild rabbits for Mr. Thomas Austin, who owned property at Barwon Park, near Geelong. They were not kept in cages as pets, but let out on the property. Mr. Austin wanted to chase them and shoot them for sport.

"Thousands of people have been chasing them all over Australia ever since, but not for sport," said Summers savagely.

"Do you know, Jack," he continued gravely, "that six years after Mr. Austin got those 24 wild rabbits and let them loose, he killed over 20,000, and judged that there were still about 10,000 running about?"

"It doesn't surprise me very much," said Howard. "I know how fast rabbits can breed."

"Mr. Austin found that out. As you know, each mother rabbit has, on the average, five kittens, but the number varies from one to as high as ten, according to the goodness or badness of the season. Then each mother rabbit has about six families a year. From those rabbits in Victoria so long ago sprang the millions that now infest practically the whole of Australia."

Summers smiled grimly.

"Jack," he said, "let me tell you something that would be funny if it were not so tragic. Just after the first rabbits came to Victoria, a man named Mr. John Robertson, who had property at Glen Alvie, took another man to the Police Court at Colac and charged him with having killed a rabbit. That unfortunate man, Jack, was fined £10 for shooting one of Mr. Robertson's rabbits."

"I can hardly believe it," exclaimed the astonished Heward.

"I admit it is hard to swallow, but it is an historical fact. But the story does not finish there. A few years after the man was fined, Robertson spent over £5,000 trying to kill off the rabbits on his property!"

"It is amazing," cried Howard. "Most interesting too. But how did the rabbits spread?"

"My grandfather told me that from Mr. Austin's property at Barwon Park they spread in every direction. They went all over Victoria and crossed the Murray River into New South Wales and South Australia. Within a few years they had covered thousands of square miles of New South Wales and had reached Queensland.

"My father," went on Summers, "had a property right out west in N.S.W. The country was wonderful, especially when it rained. Don't let people tell you that what they call the Australian desert is not fertile. When rain falls that country can become covered with grass and flowers almost overnight. Unfortunately it does not rain very often.

"But I am wandering from my story. My father had this property out there before the rabbits came, and he did well out of it. Then some rabbits appeared, to be followed by others. They commenced breeding at once. They ate the grass, the shrubs and the bushes. They ringbarked the large trees and ate millions of young plants and trees. They ate everything that was eatable and finished up eating the very heart out of the country. My father was a lot to blame. He did not take strong measures against the pests as soon as they began to arrive. He used to say that the drought was the worst enemy of rabbits and that it would kill them all off. It certainly killed millions all over the country, but thousands were left to carry on.

"My dad did a bit of poisoning, but it was not enough. He relied too much on the drought to do the work he should have done himself—or at least helped to do. Finally he had to give up his ruined land. He handed it over to the rabbits to eat what remained, and that was precious little."

Summers paused to light his pipe which had long since gone out.

"Do you realise, Jack," he continued when his pipe was drawing satisfactorily again, "that most of the barren plains and sandhills are caused by rabbits? They eat the soil bare of everything. Then the winds sweep away the red sandy surface soil and nothing will grow at all. I hate rabbits, but I hate a great deal more the foolish persons who first brought them out here."

"A lot of good can be done against them with poison," said Howard.

"Quite so, but unfortunately the poison also kills a lot of our native birds and animals," his friend pointed out.

"Including wedge-tailed eagles," grinned Howard.

"Yes, and I hope you never get old Wedge-tail with one of your beastly baits. Perhaps I am a fool, but I just do not like the idea of such a magnificent bird as that eagle being poisoned especially when he and his friends account for so many rabbits."

"If he is a lamb-killer, no death is too bad for him," said Howard stubbornly.

"Wouldn't you be prepared to let him have one lamb for every couple of hundred rabbits he killed?"

"No, I would not," said Howard shortly.

"I take it then, that you would prefer to kill all the eagles, foxes and dingoes because they take an odd lamb, and thus allow the rabbits, which they kill in hundreds, to multiply and eat all the grass, leaving none for the sheep? Why not kill the sheep too, while you're about it, and put the two of us out of a job?" grunted Summers, impatient with the obstinacy of his friend.

"Don't make such a big mountain out of such a small ant-hill," laughed Howard. He broke off suddenly. "Look, Bert," he exclaimed, "that eagle is flying off. Keep an eye on him and see where he goes."

Sitting loosely in their saddles, the stockmen watched the flight of the eagle. It attained such a height that it became a mere smudge, but the keen eyes of these bronzed outdoor men held it in view.

"See? Didn't I tell you?" exclaimed Howard triumphantly as the bird flew towards the distant peak. "It was old Wedge-tail! Bless the cheeky thing! I wonder why he must come over here each lambing season to spy on us?"

"Because he is a most ferocious lamb-killer and he is only awaiting his chance to sweep down and eat half-a-dozen," said Summers with a laugh.

"You are probably right," replied Howard, on whom his friend's sarcasm was quite lost.

Wedge-tail, unhurriedly making for his eyrie and lookout, and blissfully unaware that he had been the subject of a grim conversation, was feeling, for him, quite peaceful.

He had not been surveying that sheep run in the hope of picking up a lamb. The fact that during the past few years he had flown over the paddock at lambing time was a coincidence that had nothing to do with the lambs themselves.

Indeed, it was not so much a coincidence as a matter of routine. Wedge-tail and his mate, when nesting and family-raising were over each year, ranged far and wide. They returned at the same time each breeding season, and after establishing that their eyrie still existed, Wedge-tail always prospected the hunting grounds while his mate attended to the new lining of the eyrie. Should any heavier building work be required, Wedge-tail would assist her on his return.

The man Howard hated him as a spy and as a suspected lamb-killer. He was neither.

On his way back that morning, he collected an unwary rabbit which he detected washing and combing its whiskers at the very entrance to its burrow. He dropped on it, grabbed it, rose with it in his talons and continued his flight to the eyrie, intending to share the morsel with his mate if she wanted it.

Still at peace with the world, he arrived at the eyrie and, settling on the eating platform—a cleared space at the rim of the ledge—dropped the limp bundle of fur. Of his mate there was no sign. No doubt she was away collecting odd bits of material for the eyrie.

Not desiring the rabbit to go to waste, Wedge-tail ate it. Then he took off again and circled high above the tree. He remained in the air for a few minutes and then swooped down to his lookout in a lazy loop.

His surprise was complete when he found the branch

already occupied. Another eagle was there, and it was not his mate!

Alighting on the bough at the side of this stranger, Wedge-tail glared at him dumb-founded. The other eagle returned the stare and for a few seconds they took stock of each other. Wedge-tail saw a bird as large as himself, but much younger. But what was it doing here? This lookout and that eyrie down below belonged to him and his mate. They had established it years before. No interloper was going to intrude upon their privacy and get away unscathed.

With a scream of concentrated hatred, Wedge-tail sidled along the bough and made a fierce stab at the stranger with his beak. The stranger also screamed, beat his wings and leapt at Wedge-tail, his talons raking that bird's breast. Angrily Wedge-tail gave back a pace and then suddenly launched himself into the air, followed by a scream of derision from the stranger who was already congratulating himself on his easy victory.

But he did not know Wedge-tail. A tree branch, no matter how big, was not a fitting arena for a life-and-death struggle, and that is what Wedge-tail meant the coming fight to be. For he was angrier than he had been for many days.

High into the air he climbed, still screaming his hate, while the younger bird, in complete possession of the limb, screamed back insults at him.

Now an intelligent eagle would have had more sense than that. This stranger was young and not very bright.

No eagle with any brains at all would have deliberately appropriated another's lookout right over his eyrie. It was looking for trouble, and trouble came swiftly on the wings of a feathered hurricane.

Wedge-tail on the ground or standing on the limb of a tree was an ungainly bird, but Wedge-tail in the air was complete master of himself. From where he circled he could not see the lookout limb because it was obscured by foliage, but he knew exactly where it was situated.

Hovering on silent wings for a few seconds, his eyes darting shafts of hatred, he speared down at full speed and, shooting past the tree-top, came up under it in a perfect-timed semi-circle, talons widespread and outstretched.

The stranger saw him for a second only before he struck and then, literally knocked flying, went head-over-claws backwards, with Wedge-tail's talons still gripping his breast and Wedge-tail's hooked beak slashing at his face.

In a whirling heap of feathers, the two birds crashed clean into the eyrie, Wedge-tail on top. Flat on his back, the stranger-bird beat his wings and scratched with his claws in an effort to beat Wedge-tail off, but that experienced bird was efficiently at work with his own beak, talons and battering wings.

Harsh screams tore the air and feathers flew in all directions as if somebody were emptying a pillow case. The eyrie was large, but not large enough for a struggle like this. Sticks, small logs, twigs, branches, dead leaves, grass and rubbish became dislodged and tangled up with the fighting birds, interfering with their blows, their scratchings, rippings and tearings.

The more they struggled the worse it became and at length, with most of the eyrie pulled down over them, they were forced to stop fighting. Big sticks and little sticks almost covered them and poked into their bodies from all sides. Dried leaves, crushed to powder, clogged their eyes and their beaks. It was an inglorious end, but nothing was left for them to do but to struggle free of the wreckage.

Wedge-tail was first out. He dragged himself free of the mess, beat his wings to free them of rubbish, and then leaped to the lookout limb where he began to take stock of himself. The damage was negligible. He had lost a few feathers and had a few minor wounds.

Satisfied, he glared down at the eyrie and watched his opponent haul himself out of the broken wood-heap. The stranger, considerably bedraggled, with half his breast feathers now scattered to the four winds, and a considerable portion of his distinguishing wedge-tail buried somewhere beneath the wrecked eyrie, had all the fight knocked out of him. Wedge-tail could keep his lookout, his eyrie, his mate and, if he wanted it, the whole of the surrounding plains. He, himself, had had more than enough for one day.

Swaying uncertainly on the feeding platform for a moment and not daring to look up at Wedge-tail, he rose, a little wobbly, into the air, and steered himself unsteadily above the level of the tree-top. All he desired now was the opportunity to put as many miles as possible between himself and the menace in the tree.

But he was not going to escape as easily as all that!

Wedge-tail gave him enough time to reach cruising height and then took after him. Dropping from the limb, he made his usual upward semicircular swoop and went after the fleeing stranger like an arrow from a bow. The other eagle did not know he was being chased until Wedge-tail dropped on him from above and kicked him in the back.

Then Wedge-tail showed his real contempt for the unfortunate lookout-borrower. Round and round him he circled horizontally, and round and round him he swooped in a perpendicular loop-the-loop. At times he got above the other and dropped on his back, pushing him some yards earthwards and inflicting slight damage on him at each swoop.

The fleeing eagle, of course, did his best to avoid these attacks, but the almost total loss of his necessary wedge-tail made manouvering out of the question. He could, therefore, depend only upon the strength and speed of his wings, and these did not do him justice. He was a battered bird with no will at all to fight back.

Wedge-tail could have killed him with ease, but some twist in his character made him treat his defeated young enemy as a plaything. He followed the dejected bird for quite a distance, heaping indignities upon him and then, observing his mate to westward, wheeled off to join her, leaving the thankful lookout-borrower to fly away in peace to nurse his wounds and grow another tail.

Wedge-tail's mate was carrying a huge tuft of grass in her talons to be used as lining for the eyrie. Little did she know of the unpleasant shock that was in store for her when she reached the eyrie.

Only an hour previously she had left it in perfect condition, except for a little necessary cleaning up. Like a human husband in similar circumstances, Wedge-tail might have quite a little bit of explaining to do!

CHAPTER VI

TRAGEDY ON THE PLAINS

IN due course of time, the eyrie having been repaired, and with domestic peace prevailing on the mountain top, Wedge-tail became the proud father of another pair of fluffy young ivory-beaked eaglets. He and his devoted mate taught them the lore of the wild in the approved wedge-tail fashion, and no outstanding events occurred during the early lives of the youngsters.

But not long before they were due to leave the eyrie to live their own lives free from parental control, something did occur-something that had a most important bearing upon the future of each of the four.

One afternoon a strange eagle sailed over the range from distant parts and killed a lamb in a distant corner of the big sheep run. There was no room for doubt. Both Jack Howard and Bert Summers had witnessed the distressing affair, but at such a distance as prevented them from saving the ill-fated lamb.

That night, under the distressed eyes of Summers and the approving gaze of his six-year-old son, Peter, Jack Howard took down his big rifle and began to clean it.

His intention, he said grimly, was to ride, before dawn, to the solitary peak that held Wedge-tail's eyrie, and to return with the bird's wedge-tail as a trophy. That eagle, he told Summers, would kill no more lambs.

To his friend's suggestion that it might have been some other eagle, Howard turned a deaf ear. To him an eagle was an eagle and wedge-tail was his pet abomination. Had not Wedge-tail spied continually upon the paddock in which the lamb had been killed?

"I'll shoot him," he said grimly. "If more lambs are taken after that, then it will be just too bad for Wedge-tail."

"It will be a bit late in the day to apologise to Wedge-tail for having thought wrong of him," Summers pointed out.

"The day has yet to come when I'll apologise to any eagle, dead or alive," said Howard.

"My dad is always right," put in young Peter. "If he doesn't kill the bad old eagle, I will with my airgun."

"Good for you, son!" exclaimed his father, patting him on the head. "But don't worry. Your father never misses his aim."

"They call him Dead Shot Dick in these parts," said Summers sarcastically.

Dawn was just breaking rosily in the eastern skies as Howard and Summers rode away from the homestead in the direction of the distant peak. Howard carried a rifle, but his friend was unarmed. He had not wanted to make the trip, but Howard had persuaded him.

At precisely the same moment as the two men left the homestead, Wedge-tail and his family were preparing for an early morning hunt. The two eaglets were now almost as large as their parents. The sun was just making its appearance above the low ranges as Wedge-tail soared into the sky, followed by his mate and one eaglet. The other youngster, which had been moping a little for several days, did not follow them. When they were out of sight, he left the eyrie and flew unsteadily to the lookout. There he perched soberly, and there he was perched when the two men rode up.

Reining his horse to a halt. Howard spoke in a low voice. "There he is, Bert, up in that tree. See him? Perched on that big limb."

"How do you know it is Wedge-tail?" asked Summers.

"Of course it is he," said Howard impatiently. "You're always repeating the same old song! How do I know it was Wedge-tail who did this! How do I know it was Wedge-tail who did that! You make me tired! How do I know it is he? Isn't this his eyrie?"

"I suppose so," grunted Summers. "And you'd better look out he doesn't take to you. I'm surprised that he has remained so still."

"Might be a bit off colour," said Howard. "So much the better for me."

The two stockmen sat on their horses about two hundred feet below where the eaglet was perched. It saw them, but being unfamiliar with humans, and also being a rather sick bird, did nothing.

"For the last time, Jack," said Summers appealingly, "I ask you to leave him alone. Give him the benefit of the doubt. You have no proof that he killed that lamb."

"Watch this, Bert," replied Howard, completely disregarding his friend's plea. "It's a sitting shot. I'm not even going to get off the horse. A man can't miss at this range."

As he raised the rifle, he did not notice, high above the tree-top, three small dots growing larger every second. His whole attention was concentrated on Wedge-tail's son on the lookout branch.

There was a sharp report, which echoed and re-echoed among the hills, and the eaglet, shot clean through the head, came tumbling like a big feathered ball, to the rocky earth, to land a few yards away from the men on horseback.

"Got him!" shouted Howard gleefully. "He'll kill no more lambs. He's as dead as that lamb he killed yesterday."

"He's dead, anyway," said Summers sadly.

"Well, I'll just get off the old horse and collect his wedge-tail. It will make a fine trophy for young Peter to keep," said Howard, preparing to dismount.

He had hardly freed one foot from the stirrup iron when there came a mighty rush of wings which disintegrated the air like a miniature whirlwind.

Screaming with hatred, Wedge-tail and his mate, acting as one, were on him with beak and claw. Wedge-tail, talons crooked like steel clutches, struck him a heavy blow on the back, while his mate landed on the horse's head and, with claws tangled in the animal's mane, beat it about the ears and head with heavy wings.

Terrified, the horse gave a loud whinny and dashed off

at top speed. Howard, clinging wildly to the saddle with one hand, tried to beat off the two savage birds with the other. He had dropped the rifle at the first onslaught and it fell unheeded across the body of the dead eaglet.

Over the wide plains they rushed, Howard and his horse with two enraged eagles attacking them, and Summers riding madly after them to give what assistance he could. Then he struck trouble on his own account when he was forced to ward off the attack of the remaining eaglet.

The young bird dropped on his shoulders and clung there tenaciously. Summers dragged his horse to a stop and, turning his body with a deft twist, punched the eagle with both fists. With a surprised scream, it threw itself into the air and made towards the eyrie with all speed.

Then disaster overtook the unfortunate Howard. His horse, unable to see where it was going with the female eagle obscuring its vision with battering pinions, dashed wildly into an old stump. Howard, unprepared for this, was thrown heavily to the ground, his body striking an outcrop of rock.

Disconcerted by this rapid sequence of events, Wedge-tail and his mate withdrew from the attack and, after circling once over the scene of the disaster, returned to their eyrie.

When Summers reached his friend he could see he was in a serious condition. Apart from his torn clothes and lacerated back and face, his right leg appeared to be broken. He probably had some fractured ribs also.

A low moan that escaped the lips of his stricken comrade sent Summers hurriedly to his side. He knelt down and lifted Howard's shoulders from the hard earth.

"How is it, Jack?" he inquired anxiously.

"I'm afraid my leg is broken, Bert," groaned Howard. "You'll have to leave me here and go for assistance."

"But those eagles might return, Jack," protested Summers. "In your present state you could not fight off the three of them."

"I'll be all right," gasped the injured man. "If you can get me under that patch of saltbush over there I'll be safe. They could never get at me there. Pity I lost my rifle, but it would be too risky for you to go back and get it."

"I think I can get you to those bushes. It is only a few yards. You will be safe enough there. Then I'll ride full speed to the homestead. I'll get a few of the hands to come out with a cart for you, and I'll also send a message to the Flying Doctor. This is a job for him, of course. He can get here in a few hours."

"I'm not going to any hospital in a plane," groaned Howard. "I don't like hospitals and I don't like planes."

"Perhaps you won't have to," said Summers soothingly. "Now, come on. Easy does it, old boy. We'll soon have you comfortable under those bushes. Thank goodness the sun is not yet high enough to cause you discomfort."

With a great deal of trouble, Bert Summers managed to half-carry and half-drag his friend to the saltbush clump.

He took off his coat and placed it under Howard's head and then, finding a big stick, laid it near him. It would do to beat off any attacks should the eagles come. That accomplished, he bade Howard a cheery farewell, sprang on his horse and rode off at top speed.

Both men had wasted their time in taking precautions against further attack by the three eagles. Wedge-tail and his mate, in assailing Howard, had done something unusual; for it is only on the rarest occasions that eagles attack human beings. But then Wedge-tail was a rare type of eagle.

Back at his lookout, he planed gently to the ground and examined the body of his dead son. He waddled round it and nudged it. The rifle intrigued him and he attempted to lift it with his beak. Finding it heavy, he contented himself with slewing it round and letting it fall clear of the eaglet's body. His mate and their other youngster, a female eaglet, watched him from the lookout, where presently he joined them.

The three birds sat there quietly for a long time, scarcely moving. How long they would have emulated statues had they not been disturbed, is hard to say. But they were disturbed.

The distraction was provided by half a dozen big crows which, karking loudly, came swiftly across the plains and alighted in the tree above the eagles' heads. They stayed there for a few seconds and then, one by one, dropped to the ground to take charge of the dead eaglet. In next to no time they were fighting and swearing over the body.

This was more than Wedge-tail could stand. This act of desecration under the very eyes of the sky monarch was really too much.

When he hit the ground a few feet from them, the crows ignored him. They were not afraid of any eagle that breathed. Neither did they anticipate any aggression on the part of this one. To the crows eagles were mere providers of meals. When they killed their prey and had eaten all they required, the remainder automatically became the property of the crows. In the present case, these six black devils actually thought that the eagles had very hospitably provided one of their own bodies in order that six crows might lunch royally and well.

Disillusionment came swiftly to those six ill-mannered bush undertakers as they tore at the feathers of the dead eaglet, for Wedge-tail, with a big hop, landed squarely in their midst. With huge feathered legs astride his dead son, he roared at them and beat his wings with dark menace.

Astounded at what they regarded as highly improper behaviour, the crows drifted like black snowflakes to the tree above and filled the air with discordant and protesting karks. Wedge-tail, wings half-folded, maintained his protective pose and awaited their return. That they would be back, he had not the slightest doubt.

Like evil ink blobs from a demon's pen, they dropped down, one by one, to form a circle round him. Their wicked white eyes staring and their unlovely voices never silent, they sought to overawe the eagle and drive him away so that they could resume their interrupted feast. Wedge-tail did not trouble to answer their insults, but maintained his dignified pose.

One crow, more daring than his fellows, hopped a little closer. Wedge-tail lunged at him with his hooked beak and the crow, with a sneering squawk, hopped out of range. Another tried the same game and was driven back; but while Wedge-tail was engaged with the two in front, the others, sidling out of his direct vision, made a concerted rear attack.

Whirling round on them, the eagle beat his wings and they gave back a little, enabling the first two to sneak in closer. This game went on until Wedge-tail got tired of being assailed from all quarters, and decided to take stronger measures. Leaving the body of his son, he took to the air and, climbing rapidly to diving height, paused. What he anticipated would happen, did happen, for, no sooner had he left the earth than the six crows rushed the dead eaglet.

He waited until they were completely engrossed in their unpleasant pastime and then hurled himself earthwards with all the speed of which he was capable. With talons distended, he landed right on top of the squabbling ebony mass, flattening two of them completely under his claws and knocking two more spinning with his beating wings. The remaining two, cawing with terror, fled wildly across the open plains.

Wedge-tail made short work of the two black devils under his talons and then turned his attention to the other pair. One, with a broken wing, was fluttering and squawking loudly among the stones nearby. The other was lying, apparently unconscious, a few feet away. The eagle landed on the broken-winged crow with both feet and he, too, ceased to exist. Then, waddling across to the unconscious one, the huge bird sent him into complete oblivion with his big beak.

Honour and dignity amply satisfied, for the moment at least, Wedge-tail rose serenely and joined his impassive family on the lookout limb. Neither his mate nor their remaining eaglet had taken any part in the battle with the crows. They had not the passionate hatred of the scavengers so thoroughly possessed by their lord.

It was several hours afterwards that the three birds witnessed an interesting episode. By now the events of the morning, when Jack Howard had broken his leg, were but a dim memory, but the recollection returned with force when they saw, in the distance, a cloud of dust that presently hardened into a horse and cart.

As the birds watched from their place of vantage in the tree, they saw the cart stop near the saltbush, about a quarter of a mile away, and two men get down from it. The men bent down and appeared to be talking to the saltbush. Strange were the ways of these queer humans, thought Wedge-tail.

The owner of the station, Fred Gardiner, had returned with Bert Summers to succour the injured Howard.

"It won't be long now, Jack, before we get you out of this place," said Summers cheerily. "We got in touch by pedal wireless with the Flying Doctor, and he should be here any time. With his plane he can do the 150 miles in an hour or so. He gave instructions not to disturb you or try to cart you to the homestead. I described the country and he says he can land the plane very close to here. He has landed it in worse places, you know."

"That's good news, Bert," groaned Howard. "I've had a pretty anxious time since you have been away."

As they made him comfortable on a feather mattress they had brought, and erected a small tent over the saltbush to keep off the fierce rays of the sun, he described the episode of the eagles and the crows.

"I could not see all that was going on, but every time that eagle screamed and the crows karked back at him, I thought they were all coming after me."

"Nothing to worry about now, Jack," soothed Summers. "Just take it quietly. The doctor won't be long."

"Bert," said Howard with a grunt of pain. "I'm sure that was Wedge-tail who attacked me. I didn't shoot the old wretch after all."

"No. Apparently you got one of his youngsters."

"He will keep. I won't have this broken leg always," gasped the injured man.

"Well, don't go worrying about Wedge-tail now," advised Summers. "Try to get him off your mind for a while."

From their tree, the three eagles watched the scene with interest, wondering what the big white thing was that had mysteriously appeared and covered the saltbush. They had never seen a tent erected before. Wedge-tail was half-inclined to sail over and have a closer look, but did not have the necessary energy.

At his side, his mate was beginning to grow restless, and presently she flew off, followed a few seconds later by the eaglet. Wedge-tail let them go. He intended to stay there and watch those mad humans.

High in the blue, his mate and their daughter inspected the terrain in search of prey; and as there was no sign of the crows returning, and no movement from the men or their tent, Wedge-tail relaxed. But though he was half-asleep, his keen ears were alert for any unusual sounds.

Thus it was that, borne on the slight warm breeze, there came to him a sound he had never heard before. It was a gentle purr that gradually grew louder.

Opening his eyes, he gazed at the sky. His family was still there, but, far away to the left, he saw another bird. It was not an eagle.

Then what was the thing? Wedge-tail sat up and began to take notice. This was larger by far than any bird he had ever seen and it was making that purring noise.

This thing, Wedge-tail considered, called for immediate investigation, and within a few seconds he was air-borne and climbing swiftly to join his mate and daughter. He approached them from the right and the strange bird from the left. It was terrific, this stranger, and the noise it was now making was ear-shattering. If that bird was an eagle, then it was the patron saint, the father, of the whole species. It was a monster.

Dr. Grahame, at the control of the Flying Medical Service plane, was watching the ground for the white flag he had told Summers to wave, and did not see the eagles until something dark flashed across the front of the plane.

Glancing quickly upwards, he saw Wedge-tail circling and taking stock of him. As long as the bird stayed there, it would be all right. The doctor did not want to collide with it.

Looking earthwards again, he saw the white signal flag waving from a wide open space. It appeared to be an ideal landing place, and the doctor commenced to circle so as to come down against the slight breeze.

Then it happened. A dark mass suddenly blotted out his view, there was a terrific scream and a terrible flurry as if dark brown snowflakes were enveloping the plane. A roar and a rattle told the doctor what had occurred. An eagle had collided with the plane and had shattered the propeller, tearing itself to pieces in doing so.

Widely-experienced in the handling of aeroplanes in all circumstances, the Flying Doctor looked anxiously downwards for a good spot in which to make a forced landing. Fortunately, he had almost completed his circle before the eagle struck the machine, and was, therefore, in a favourable position to reach the ground at the spot indicated by Summers and his waving flag.

With a sure and steady hand, the Flying Doctor guided the injured plane downwards and landed it safely on the hard earth. As he climbed out to greet Summers and Gardiner, he smiled grimly.

"You men certainly planned an exciting welcome for me," he said.

"By jingo, doctor, that was a narrow escape you had!" exclaimed Summers. "I thought you would crash when that eagle struck your plane. Did the thing deliberately attack you?"

"I didn't see it, but I hardly think so," the doctor answered. "No doubt it was just investigating me and wondering what strange manner of bird I was. Then the propeller struck it and reduced the eagle population by one."

"There were three of them," put in Gardiner. "Two were flying almost together and it was one of those that struck you. The other one flew away. The third one was up above you all the time, and is still there."

"I'll take your word for it. Now, where is the patient?" asked the doctor briskly.

"In the tent over there," answered Gardiner, and led the way across.

As the Flying Doctor made his way to the saltbush he said ruefully, "I'm in a bit of a hole now. That eagle broke the propeller and I haven't got a spare one with me, of course. I'll have to send a message to the base for assistance. Will the plane be safe here for the time being?"

"I think so. Perhaps we could send over some horses and have it towed to the homestead for greater safety?" suggested Summers.

"It would be better. In the meantime, let us get our patient fixed up and ready to transfer there," and the doctor bent down and crawled under the tent as he spoke.

A dot in the sky above them, Wedge-tail was a seething mass of feathered fury. Had he not seen that new and monstrous bird attack his mate and literally tear her to shreds? Had he not seen his daughter flee in such terror from the monster that it was most unlikely that he would ever see her again? Had not his son, earlier in the day, been killed by a mad human being?

Just what sort of a bird was that thing down there? Unless his eyes had played him false, and they never had done so before, he had actually seen a man come out of its body. What manner of bird was large enough and strong enough to carry a man?

With these thoughts coursing through his brain, Wedge-tail's fury became tempered with a slight doubt and a slight fear, and he hesitated to carry out his plan to attack the thing. No, before he did anything like that, a lot of hard thinking had to be done.

Big as this strange bird was, however, it could not possibly alight in his lookout tree, and because he did his thinking best at his lookout, he quietly and unobtrusively planed down to it, taking up a position where he could keep a watchful eye on the monster and upon the unwelcome humans.

Twilight stealing quietly across the plains still found him there. The men, the tent and the horse and cart had long since departed, but the bird had not.

Climbing big and silver into the velvet sky, the large old moon sent its pale beams stealing far and wide until they were lost in the vastness of the dim horizon, but, pale as they were, the shafts of silver were sufficiently luminous to show Wedge-tail the outlines of that strange slayer of his beloved mate, perched silently on the ground in the distance.

CHAPTER VII
THE TRAIL OF VENGEANCE

FAR away at the station homestead, the Flying Doctor had attended to Jack Howard's broken leg and other injuries, which were not serious, and had made the stockman comfortable in his quarters. The leg injury proved to be a simple fracture, and the doctor assured Howard that, under the care of his wife, and with occasional visits by himself, it would not be long before the patient would again be riding the runs.

This, of course, greatly cheered the Howards. Little Peter was impatient to learn all about the bad wicked eagle that had hurt his father, and would have pestered the injured man had he not been shooed out of the sick room. Gently, but firmly, Bert Summers took the little boy away and, seated outside under a large old gum tree, told him all about it.

Little Peter seethed with indignation.

"I will take my airgun and go right away out there and shoot that nasty old eagle," he said determinedly, doubling one small fist and punching the palm of his other hand with it. "That bird isn't going to hurt my daddy like that!"

Summers smiled down at the lad's serious little face.

"I'm afraid your airgun would not do much harm to such a big bird as Wedge-tail, Peter," he said gently. "Anyway, you must remember that your dad shot the eagle's little boy and the father bird was only paying your dad out."

Little Peter gave this aspect of the matter very grave consideration for a few seconds.

"I suppose, maybe, that is true, Uncle Bert," he said at last, giving Summers his pet title, and one which the stockman cherished, "but eagle birds are nasty old things that kill our lambs; so my daddy was right when he killed the little eagle so that it would not grow up into a real big one and kill more lambs."

"I don't think that poor old eagle will kill any more lambs around here, Peter," said Summers, smiling down on the sturdy little bush boy. "You see, he has lost all his family now, so I think he is almost certain to fly right away and live in some other part of the country, never to come back here again."

"Do you think he will fly away before tomorrow morning, Uncle Bert?" asked the lad anxiously.

"Well, now, that is more than I can say. He might be gone by now."

"I hope not. I hope he stays right in his old tree until to-morrow, because I am going to go out there with my airgun and shoot him dead," replied little Peter with great determination.

"Well, well, Peter boy, we'll see about that in the morning. Now, run along inside and have your tea. And don't go worrying your dad. He is very sick, you know," warned the stockman.

"I won't, Uncle Bert. Good night," said the boy.

As he ran off into the house, Bert Summers gazed after him affectionately. He loved the lad, as did everyone at the station, and would do anything in the world for him. He was glad that Peter had not asked him to go out and destroy Wedge-tail.

Rising to his feet and stretching himself, he strolled into the homestead where he found the Flying Doctor talking to Gardiner.

"I'll have to stay the night with you, Mr. Gardiner," Dr. Grahame was saying as Summers entered. "I arranged over the pedal wireless for a new propeller to be sent and I hope that another plane will arrive with it in the morning. I suppose my machine will be safe out on the plains? Nothing likely to damage it, is there?"

"Nothing, except a sudden storm, and we are not likely to have one at this time of the year," the station owner assured him. "As for staying the night, we are more than delighted to have you. We get so few visitors, you know."

"Thank you very much," replied the Flying Doctor. "I hope you are right about the plane. Do you think we should go out there now and peg it down with ropes, in case a storm should blow up in the night?"

"It is quite unnecessary, doctor, I assure you," said Gardiner. "By daybreak the men will be there with a team of horses to tow it in. The repair job might take longer than you think, and can be done better here."

"Quite so," agreed Dr. Grahame.

Until bed time, the doctor entertained Gardiner and Summers with interesting stories of his medical work in the outback in association with the famous Australian Inland Mission, telling them of the many different types of cases he and his fellow Flying Doctors were called upon to handle.

The first kookaburra had not greeted the glory of the dawn before preparations were completed for the journey to the stranded aeroplane. Dr. Grahame, Gardiner and Summers snatched a hasty cup of tea before climbing into the cart, which Summers drove, two strong old draught-horses plodding along behind.

"Well, doctor, it is still there, and looks as if it is in one piece," said Summers cheerfully, as they neared the machine.

"Excellent!" replied the Flying Doctor, jumping to the ground as soon as the cart stopped. While Gardiner and Summers unloaded the hauling gear, he walked briskly over to the aeroplane to give it a more careful examination. What he saw satisfied him, and he returned to the cart to give the other two men a hand.

Returning from his early morning hunt, Wedge-tail, while still a long distance away, noted the activity, and, arriving overhead, but keeping at a great height, sailed in a slow circle to observe what was going on.

Untying the two draught-horses from the rear of the cart, Summers and Gardiner, assisted by the doctor, adjusted the harness and hauling gear and then attached it to the tail-end of the plane. This completed to their satisfaction, and tested by a trial haul of a few yards, Gardiner got into the cart to drive it back to the homestead. The doctor and

Summers would accompany the disabled plane on the long weary tramp home.

Being only a light machine, the kind used by the Flying Medical Service, the task was a fairly easy one for the sturdy horses. The ground, except for patches of saltbush and other stunted growth, was bare and the surface fairly level. By exercising care and judgment in dodging obstructions, they made good progress.

From his vantage-point in the heavens, Wedge-tail watched their departure with hard, unwinking eyes. So those men were taking away his gigantic enemy, were they? Very interesting, but no more interesting than that queer bird itself, with its lack of feathers. Wedge-tail threw a scornful glance at the departing plane being towed away across the plains, and told himself that he would like to see any human beings or their horses try to pull him along the ground by the tail.

He watched the scene below for a minute or two, and then flew off to his eyrie.

It was slow work for the men and horses removing the damaged machine, and they were not out of sight before Wedge-tail again took to the air. Such events, being outside the ordinary daily routine, were very interesting and kept life from becoming dull and prosaic, but they did not bring food to the eyrie, and the eagle, though he had breakfasted off two young rabbits, was feeling hungry again.

This time he did not go towards his usual hunting ground, but sailed over the low mountain range behind the solitary peak. Young kangaroos and rabbits were excellent food, but his appetite craved a change of diet. Though he had not seen anything of the kind in these particular parts, there was no telling whether a dingo pup, or possibly a fox, was not to be had among those hills.

During the hundreds of miles he had covered in between the breeding seasons, he had met and found himself more than a match for dingoes, provided they were young ones. Foxes, however, were wily animals and were not profitable game for an eagle that was pressed for time. Patience and lots of time were necessary in securing a fox. Wedge-tail had never wasted much of either upon them in the past, except when he was not very hungry and hunted them just as a game of skill.

His prospecting of the hills was not productive at all. He saw nothing interesting, save a hardy old wallaroo which was squatting on a craggy ridge and looking like a stout pig.

He left the hills and circled wide over the plains, deciding to lunch off the inevitable rabbit. It was not long before he sighted two of them. They were lying in the shade of a leopardwood tree. He caught one, killed it and fed off it in the very shade of the leopardwood, and then took his leisurely way back to the lookout. It had been a dull, routine hunt.

During his wide sweep over the plains, he had noticed the horses and the aeroplane which, enveloped in a small cloud of dust, were slowly nearing the homestead. He was, for a brief moment, tempted to spear down and try conclusions with the strange bird, but better counsels prevailed, and he returned to his lookout to doze in the warm sunshine.

Tired and dusty, Dr. Grahame and Summers eventually

reached the homestead, and while they were unharnessing the horses, Gardiner, who had arrived in the cart long before them, came to the Flying Doctor with a message that had come over the pedal wireless.

Dr. Mason, who was to have flown out with the new propeller, had received an emergency call to go to a case over 200 miles from the Gardiner property. After attending it, he would come on with the propeller.

"It will mean a delay of hours," said Dr. Grahame with a touch of irritation. "If the case Mason is attending is serious, he might have to transport a patient back to the base. If that happens, goodness only knows when we will see him."

"It is a wonder they go to such trouble and expense," ventured Summers. "Why didn't they send out the propeller on a truck as soon as they got your message?"

"Time is a most important factor in our work," the Flying Doctor told him. "Even now, my services might be needed urgently hundreds of miles from here, and I'm forced to twiddle my thumbs in idleness."

The sable fingers of darkness were reaching out to enclose the plains in their velvet clutches when an urgent message arrived from Dr. Mason. As Grahame had feared, Mason had been held up. The case he had attended had not been a transport one, but while attending it he had received orders over the radio to fly inland to where a party of prospectors were suffering from the effects of poisoned water. That being so, he could not possibly go to the assistance of the disabled plane at Gardiner's that day.

"Persons who poison water in this country where it is so scarce should be shot," said Grahame angrily, as he read the message a second time. "If they must do it to kill off rabbits, they should be forced to place notices at the waterholes saying that the water is not fit for human beings to drink."

"Most of them do," said Gardiner. "I'm afraid you must make the best of the delay, doctor. This station is your home for as long as you care to stay."

"I know that, and thanks very much, Mr. Gardiner," replied the doctor. "But this delay is most irritating. I'm a reasonable man and I'm a nature lover too; but at the present moment I'd kill every wedge-tailed eagle of which I could get within shooting distance."

"I'll help you, doctor," piped up an eager small voice, and the three men turned to observe young Peter.

The Flying Doctor's face broke into a quick smile as he patted the boy's head and told him not to be quite so blood-thirsty.

Before darkness took complete charge, Gardiner, Summers and Grahame, under the watchful eyes and loud directions of young Peter, saw that the damaged plane was securely roped and pegged down against the possibility of a sudden windstorm. Little Peter took the job seriously, and though the smiling men did not carry out the orders he gave, it filled him with a great sense of importance to shout out instructions to the working men.

Following a cheer-up visit to Jack Howard, Gardiner, Summers and their visitor retired early that night. But Dr.

Grahame could not sleep. He was restless and impatient over his enforced stay at the homestead. He tossed and turned on his bed, and when dawn's first faint gleam lightened his room, he realised that it was quite impossible to sleep, so resolved to stroll round the station property in the clear, sweet morning air.

Having dressed, he went outside, to be greeted by the melodious notes of a pair of magpies in the old gum tree. Magpies were the Flying Doctor's favourite birds. He loved them for their boldness, their bravery and the sheer liquid beauty of their glorious voices. He paused in his walk completely to enjoy the carolling with which the hidden song birds greeted another day.

Presently, the two black-and-white artists left the tree and flew to earth, immediately to commence the all-important search for breakfast. Grubs, worms, beetles, or anything equally tasty, would meet with their warmest approval.

The Flying Doctor watched them use their powerful beaks to dig, and also as levers to turn over stones and bits of wood to get at any insects or worms that lurked beneath.

And as he observed them, Dr. Grahame shook his head with regret as he thought of the numbers of magpies that had been killed by thoughtless people, and the consequent loss to their friends, the farmers. In settled areas, many magpies had been killed for no other reason than that they were brave birds who protected their nests from small boys searching for eggs and nestlings. Golfers, too, had reduced their numbers because the birds sometimes had flown at them as they drove balls under trees containing nests. The good the magpies did in keeping the greens and fairways clear of destructive crickets, meant nothing to those hitters of the small white ball.

His thoughts running in these channels, Dr. Grahame, leaving the two bush musicians to their serious hunting, strolled round the back of the barn to where the plane stood. It was in order, so he wandered slowly down the paddock towards a small tank, or excavated waterhole, where the shrill voices of hundreds of small birds told him that they were paying their early morning visit to the life-giving water.

Clouds of little finches and parrots rose protestingly as he approached. Not desiring to interfere with them, he turned to retrace his steps to the house. Walking slowly, and enjoying the bracing air of the morning, he glanced towards the east where the sun was just appearing to start another day's work. The roseate glow of the shining disc turned a few scattered clouds into scarlet and orange, and as the doctor watched the changing colours with keen appreciation, he noticed a small moving speck.

His first impression was that this was the relief plane with his new propeller, so he quickened his pace. A keener look, however, showed him that it was not an aeroplane, but a large bird, most likely an eagle. Idly he watched its swift approach. Yes, it was a wedge-tail.

Dr. Grahame frowned. He loved all the wild creatures, but at that moment was finding it hard to love eagles.

He was perhaps two hundred yards from the homestead

when he saw the bird poised above it. That eagle, Grahame told himself quickly, must be after a chicken, a fowl, the pet cat, or something. What impudence, to actually come to the homestead! Anyway, no matter what the bird was after, he must be prevented from getting it.

As he broke into a run, the Flying Doctor saw the eagle hover on wide pinions for a second, and then dive swiftly downwards, flashing from sight behind a shed.

Immediately the doctor heard loud cackling, screeching and crowing, and as he sped round the corner of the shed, he came into full view of the station fowlyard. There, in the middle of the pen, was Wedge-tail, a half-grown cockerel under his claws. The rest of the feathered inhabitants of the yard were rushing hither and thither, dashing themselves against the low wire netting in a frantic endeavour to get away from this awful menace.

Amazement halted the doctor in his tracks for fully three seconds. Then, with an inarticulate cry of rage, he grabbed a handy piece of wood and, rushing to the wire fence, hurled it with all his strength.

The piece of wood whizzed under Wedge-tail's very beak and, with a startled scream, he sprang into the air, leaving the dead cockerel behind. As he flew off, the angry doctor rushed madly in the same direction, waving a perfectly ineffectual fist.

Wedge-tail, however, was not lingering behind for conversation, explanation or apology, but was heading at full speed for his lookout. As he neared it, fear gave place to rage as he thought of the breakfast he had lost. These interfering humans! They were almost as bad as his pet abominations, the crows.

CHAPTER VIII

THE MONARCH WINS HIS KINGDOM

DR. GRAHAME'S indignation at Wedge-tail's raid on the fowlyard was shared by everyone at the homestead, while little Peter Howard seethed with childish rage.

He was with the men as they inspected the body of the dead fowl, and then withdrew, a determined expression on his face. Running into the homestead, he reappeared within a few moments carrying his small airgun.

"Come with me doctor," he said. "We will go straight away now and kill that old eagle stone dead. He broke my father's leg and now he has killed one of Mr. Gardiner's chookies. One of his friends also ran into your aeroplane and broke its propeller. He has got to die."

The Flying Doctor's sense of humour overcame his indignation for a moment as he looked down affectionately at the determined little boy.

"You are a brave hunter, Peter, my boy," he said with a kindly smile, "but how do we know it was the same eagle? We must not go blaming birds for what they might not have done. And of course we can't blame the eagle who killed this cockerel for the accident to my plane."

"No, not for that, doctor, but of course it was the same eagle that broke my dad's leg," insisted Peter.

"I think the boy is right, doctor," put in Summers. "Old Wedge-tail is the gamest bird I know. It was his mate that smashed your propeller and got herself killed at the same time. This might be his revenge."

"What, killing a young fowl?" exclaimed the doctor. "Nothing of the kind. He has been over this homestead before and has no doubt noted the fowlyard. He paid an early morning visit before anyone was stirring, just to get an easy meal. It was bad luck for him that I happened to be around, that's all."

"Now you come to mention it, doctor, Wedge-tail might be responsible for other fowls I've missed," said Gardiner. "I've lost one or two from time to time. I thought they must have got out of the yard and wandered off down the paddocks where the foxes picked them up."

"He's no ordinary bird, that Wedge-tail." said Summers.

"He will be a dead bird if young Peter gets hold of him, won't he, my boy," asked the doctor, patting Peter on the bead.

"Yes, he will, but nobody will come and help me shoot him," complained the little boy.

"Wedge-tail will have to wait. There are more urgent things to be done right now. Later on, perhaps, we will deal with him," Bert Summers told him. Peter wrinkled up his small nose in disgust at the way these grown-ups pushed aside worthwhile aims.

"That eagle is becoming a nuisance," said the station owner, as they returned to the homestead for breakfast.

"Something will have to be done about him. It looks as if I'll have to polish up my old rifle and head for his eyrie."

"Watch out that young Peter doesn't beat you to it," laughed Dr. Grahame. "What a lovable little chap he is!"

"All of us on this station would do practically anything in the world for that boy," replied Gardiner. "He's the boss around here. You can have no idea how that kiddie has brightened up this homestead. Neither Bert nor I are married, as you know, and I have always said that there is no sweeter music round a place than a child's footsteps and merry laughter. Young Peter is king here. Ah, you can't beat kids for making a home cheerful."

"Except when they are howling babies," grinned the doctor, and the other two men laughed with him.

"Young Peter is quite unspoiled in spite of the affection we lavish on him," said Summers, as they sat down to breakfast.

Miles away, Wedge-tail, too, was sitting down to breakfast, feeding off a tasty morsel of plump rose-breasted galah—a fitting substitute for the cockerel he had lost.

On his way home from the sheep station, he had noticed a flock of galahs busily feeding on a scanty patch of grass. The hungry birds, after their natural habit, were spread out like a big fan and were all busy digging into the earth for roots and bulbs.

They must have been exceptionally hungry, for they had neglected to post the customary sentry to look out for danger. This, of course, suited Wedge-tail who, without the slightest trouble, secured the plumpest bird when he dropped unheralded into their midst. The rest of the flock flew away screaming their protests as the eagle commenced his breakfast.

It was not until just before lunch that the relief plane, piloted by Dr. Mason, arrived at the Gardiner homestead, and all hands combined to assist the two doctors, who were both able mechanics. The remnants of the broken propeller had to be removed and the new one installed and tested. Several minor repairs to the machine's undercarriage also were necessary.

The job was well advanced when the men received the cheery call to lunch.

None of them noticed the absence of young Peter. In ordinary circumstances, the boy would have been one of the busiest of the workers, super-intending the job and bossing the men around. He was first missed when his mother called out to him to come and get his lunch, and received no reply.

Now, Peter always had been a most obedient little boy. Farther advanced in the ways of the world in which he lived than any city boy twice his age, he knew full well the dangers of straying away from the homestead. He had been taught that he must never go any great distance from the house unless accompanied by an adult. The homestead people, knowing this, thought he must be playing in one of the many barns or sheds and had not heard the call for lunch.

Bert Summers, who volunteered to "round him up" as he called it, had a strange doubt in his mind. He could not forget the fact that the lad had not been watching the plane being repaired. From past experience of the boy's ways, he knew that Peter should have revelled in the experience.

Nevertheless, Summers proceeded to search all the likely places, calling the boy's name as he did so.

But there was no answering call or the sound of running feet. This was not surprising, for little Peter, his toy airgun clutched in a determined small fist, and a bottle of water and a piece of bread in his pocket, was two miles away, trudging over the burning plains in the direction of the eagle's eyrie, which was at least seven miles from the homestead.

Though an obedient boy, Peter had felt very keenly the hurt done to his father, the damage to the doctor's plane, and the death of the cockerel. He blamed Wedge-tail for it all. The adults had turned down his excellent suggestion that they should help him kill the eagle, so there had been nothing else for him to do but kill the nasty thing himself. Somebody, he kept telling himself as he plodded onwards, had to do the job.

Now, it chanced that at the same time as little Peter crept unseen from the house, a stranger to the plains was making his way down out of the low range of barren hills that stretched away behind Wedge-tail's eyrie. Wedge-tail, out on a scouting mission, observed this newcomer and was vastly interested; for dingoes were particularly rare in his territory.

But this was not a pure-bred native dog. Years before, a dingo-shooter, working far to the north of the hills, had

had as a companion a female Alsatian. This dog had proved untrue to her trust, because one night when the moon was full and the hunting dingoes were serenading it with their mournful howls, she had quietly left her owner's camp and joined the wild dog pack.

The gaunt and fiercely-hungry dog that Wedge-tail was watching was the son of this errant lady Alsatian who had returned to her master, long months after her departure, accompanied by this very son. The dingo-shooter welcomed with delight his long-lost pet, but had no great love for her half-breed son. This lack of affection was mutual and, before it was fully-grown, the mongrel Alsatian-dingo returned to the dingo pack and became absorbed in it.

Well nigh starving after a long trek across the barren hills, among which he had not sighted a thing worth eating, the large, tawny dog left the foothills and began to slink across the flat country.

He was not there from choice. On the other side of the hills he had been the leader of the pack, whose hunting grounds were far to the north. Life there had been good for a long time, and the pack had prospered.

Then bad times had come. Game got scarce and the waterholes, soaks and tanks began to dry up. This drove the pack southwards, where conditions were a little better, but still not up to the standard to which the dingoes had been accustomed. With the shortage of food came trouble. This culminated in a pitched battle between the leader and another dingo who aspired to the leadership. Victory went to the challenging native dog, and the deposed half-breed thought it wiser to leave.

An urge to see what was beyond the low ranges caused him to cross them. It took him several days, and as both food and water were almost non-existent, he was lank and lean when he reached the plains on the other side.

Poor he might be as to physical condition, but his ravenous hunger made him a terrible creature to encounter.

Wedge-tail, sailing on high and watching the dog passing from saltbush to saltbush, felt slight resentment at its arrival in his kingdom. The dog was no young pup, and Wedge-tail knew that if he attacked it he probably would have a first-class battle on his talons. But that did not worry him in the least. He had breakfasted well off rabbit and had lunched to the full on a young red kangaroo. At the moment he was not hungry, so had a complete sense of well-being.

Circling and watching, he made up his mind to attack that dog, come what may. It was a long time since he had attacked either a dingo or a fox as a test of skill, and he felt eager for the coming battle.

From his vantage-spot in the sky, Wedge-tail could see for many miles over the surrounding country, and soon sighted another figure. It looked like a small human being. What was it doing out here? Surely it did not intend to deprive him of his conquest of the dog!

If so, thought Wedge-tail, it was really too exasperating! Had not these humans done enough harm and caused him enough trouble already? What utter nuisances they were!

Little Peter, plodding steadily onwards, his wide hat shading his head from the fierce sun but not contributing much to the coolness he longed for, was already regretting his decision to kill the eagle. His small face was grimed with perspiration and swarms of flies worried him a great deal. His stout little heart, however, would not permit him to turn back after he had plodded over two miles. Having set his face to the task, he intended to see it through.

By this time consternation reigned at the homestead. Peter was definitely missing. It was Bert Summers who first realised where he might have gone, and he asked Mrs. Howard to see if the toy airgun was in its usual place. It was not.

"I believe the young devil has gone off alone to shoot old Wedge-tail, bless his heart," exclaimed the stockman. "I remember seeing him about an hour ago, so he can't be far away. Don't worry, Mrs. Howard, I'll have him back safe and sound in next to no time. And, by the way, don't let Jack know, will you? There is no need to cause him needless worry."

Leaving the anxious mother staring across the burning plains in the direction of the eagle's eyrie, Summers slung his rifle over his back, quickly mounted his horse, and prepared to leave. With a wave of the hand, he vanished in a cloud of dust, aiming straight across country and relying on his keen eyes to pick up any moving object on that flat and sparsely-covered land.

A black speck in the sky a long way off told him that Wedge-tail, or some other eagle, was on hunting business.

He hoped it was Wedge-tail, for, even if the boy did reach the foot of the mountain which bore the eyrie, Wedge-tail's absence would ensure his safety. It was extremely unlikely that the eagle would attack the little boy on the open plains; but quite possible if he were near the eyrie.

Slinking across an open space, the gaunt halfbreed dog suddenly froze in his tracks. Not a dozen yards away a fat rabbit was sheltering from the sun under a low bush. The dog crouched and tensely watched the furry animal which, instinctively becoming aware that it was not alone, looked across the sandy patch and saw the crouching dog.

Stricken motionless with terror, hypnotised by the uncanny glare in the wild dog's famished eyes, the rabbit sat like a statue and did not heed the voice of a small boy. It is doubtful if the terrified animal even heard it.

On the other side of the bush and invisible to the dog, young Peter also had seen the rabbit. He halted near the bush and, pointing his gun at the small animal, said, "I'm going to shoot you dead, rabbit."

Fascinated by the dog, which had crept a little closer, the trembling rabbit took no notice of Peter.

"I don't like you, rabbit," continued the boy. "You eat all the grass that is for the sheep. I like you better than I like eagles, but all the same I don't like you very much. That is why I'm going to shoot you, see?"

He squinted along the barrel of the gun, but a twig interrupted his clear view. He therefore moved round a little to get a better sight, and came within the dog's range of vision. Taken slightly aback, the dog crouched low to earth, but still concentrated on the rabbit. He had had some experience of the human race and was not afraid of this small specimen who, as long as he did not interfere with the rabbit, could be ignored.

High aloft, Wedge-tail watched the drama anxiously. He did not know the rabbit was under the bush. He thought the boy and the dog were interested in each other only. This added to his anxiety, and he dropped a few yards to get a better view. Bert Summers, still a long way off, noticed the manoeuvre, but did not appreciate its meaning. He had not yet seen either Peter or the wild dog.

Moving round the bush still further, Peter saw the dog for the first time. Young as he was, he knew that this was no tame old sheep dog, but a very savage creature of the wilds. It made his heart beat faster, and he stood there in hesitation, his gun clenched firmly in his hand. Then, in a very small voice, he said, "You go away, dog."

But the dog did not go away. It was there to get that rabbit and it intended to get it. No small boy was going to stop it.

Urgently hungry, it began to advance stealthily. Peter, standing quite near the terrified rabbit, edged a little to one side and as he did so, the wild dog sprang.

Flashing past him like a tawny streak, it seized the rabbit in its powerful jaws and began to worry it to death.

And then, little Peter, filled with indignation and forgetting for a moment his uneasiness, did a foolish thing. He struck the dog on the back hard with the butt of his airgun.

With rabbit's blood dripping from its slavering jaws and bits of rabbit's fur clinging to its nose, the infuriated dog whirled round and knocked the little boy flying. And as Peter lay on his back crying with terror, the dog crouched on its haunches, snarling horribly, its lips rolled back revealing two rows of terrible fangs. Muscles tensed and mad with anger, it gathered itself for a spring that would hurl its gaunt body on top of the prostrate child and bury its wicked teeth in his small throat.

But, ere that infuriated animal could spring, a screaming, feathered, steel-taloned bomb fell from the skies with a speed that would baffle sight, and buried deadly claws into its yellow back.

Then there began a fight the like of which never before had been witnessed on those arid plains. Wedge-tail, savage and relentless warrior of the skies, and the half-bred dingo, hunger-maddened, savage and relentless warrior of the earth, were locked in a death-struggle. Over and over they tumbled, yellow hide and dark brown feathers in a whirling, screaming, howling, biting, tearing and clawing mass.

Sobbing with terror, little Peter managed to sit up on the hard earth. He was within a few yards of the battling creatures, but so engrossed were they in their own affairs, that they had forgotten his existence.

Tears coursing down his face made rivulets through the grime and perspiration, but the little boy had no thought of his personal appearance. On hands and knees he crawled under the nearest saltbush and pulled it round his body as much as he could. There with the remains of the dead rabbit for company, he peered fearfully between twigs at the titanic battle between bird and beast.

Suddenly the combatants fell apart. Wedge-tail hauled himself to his feet, his feathers ruffled and his beak and talons bloodstained. The dog, blood running from wounds in his back and rips in his flanks where beak and talons had done their grim work, crouched and panted, ready for a renewal of the conflict.

The eagle, unable to take the initiative on the ground, stood firm, awaiting the onslaught he felt sure would come; and when the dog launched himself, Wedge-tail met him willingly with wings beating wildly and claws outstretched.

As the dog struck home on his breast, the eagle folded him in gigantic wings. Once again there was that whirling mass of feathers, skin and hair, while the atmosphere was torn by harsh screams and horrible snarling yelps.

From his hiding place under the bush, little Peter watched fascinated, his fear completely gone. He was, of course, wholly on Wedge-tail's side, and in his excitement began to urge his champion to greater effort.

But, so much noise were the combatants making that neither of them heard, or cared about, the low voice of a small boy saying, "Oh, you good old eagle! Bite him hard! Scratch his eyes out! Kill him dead and eat him up!"

Came another pause as the combatants separated themselves. The wild dog backed away a little and then fell into a crouch. With fangs bared in a horrible snarl, he glared at the eagle, who stood, rock firm, and glared back with hate-filled agate eyes. Wedge-tail had lost quite a number of feathers and the gaunt hide of his wild enemy was criss-crossed with wounds.

Tensing himself for another spring, but not quite so sure of himself this time, the panting dog was surprised, and greatly relieved, when Wedge-tail suddenly took to the air.

The dog's surprise was matched by that of little Peter, who, seeing the great bird take wing, crouched back into the bush to hide himself from the dog.

"The big coward," he said to himself. "Gee, I hope that old dog doesn't come looking for me again."

But the dingo had no thought of Peter. Relieved, and thinking, like the boy, that the eagle had had enough, it began to lick its wounds, whining and yelping as it did so.

Peter and the half-breed had both done Wedge-tail a grave injustice. That wily bird had not turned coward. Fighting on the ground, he was out of his element, and his return to the skies was a premeditated act that spelled doom for the wild dog below.

Thinking the fight was over, and wholly engrossed in attending to his wounds, the son of the Alsatian was quite unprepared when the next attack came.

Having gained sufficient height, Wedge-tail planed down with the speed of light, knocking the yellow beast over and over. The eagle did not land but, soaring sharply upwards again, shot down a second time, to smite his enemy with beak and talon.

The first swoop had knocked the wind completely out of the dog and had left him quite defenceless against the second. Wedge-tail's third swoop found him an easy prey. The great bird landed fairly and squarely on his gaunt frame, breaking several ribs under the sheer weight of the impact.

That was the end of the dog whose mother had been an Alsatian and whose father had been a native Australian dingo. Utterly conquered, he could do nothing to prevent the triumphant eagle ripping his throat to pieces with that huge, curved beak.

Completely enthralled by it all, little Peter, peeping through gaps in the sheltering bush, watched Wedge-tail engaged on the enjoyable recreation of having afternoon tea off the scanty body of his fallen enemy.

Presently he saw the great bird pause and stiffen into immobility. Something had distracted his attention. And then Peter heard a welcome sound—the drumming of horse's hoofs. That would be somebody from the homestead coming to look for him.

Without the slightest sign of haste or perturbation, Wedge-tail rose slowly into the heavens—swollen with dignity and half-breed dingo. As he left the scene of battle, little Peter crawled from under the bush, just as Bert Summers rode up and hastily dismounted.

"Are you all right, Peter?" he cried anxiously. "Was that Wedge-tail I saw fly away from here just now? Did he attack you? What happened to that dog lying there?"

The rapidity of the questions bewildered little Peter,

whose sole reply was, "That good old eagle saved me from being killed by that dog."

"What do you mean, Peter? What has happened?" asked the stockman anxiously.

Before replying, the boy looked skywards to where, high in the blue, the eagle was slowly circling as if he were a victorious general giving a battlefield a last survey before departing with his triumphant army.

"He's a good old eagle," Peter repeated and then proceeded to tell Summers the whole exciting story.

"Good gracious! What an experience you have had, Peter," breathed the stockman when the boy had finished. "How are you feeling now? Not scared any more?"

"No fear, Uncle Bert. All I want to do is to go home and tell my daddy that he must not harm Wedge-tail!"

"I'll be ready in a second, Peter," replied Summers, walking over and closely examining the remains of the dead dog.

"What a dreadful-looking brute," he muttered. "A half-breed. Much more dangerous than a fullblooded dingo. Young Peter certainly had a narrow escape."

Adjusting his rifle on his shoulder and gently picking the boy up, he slowly mounted his horse. When they had travelled about a quarter of a mile, Summers reined the horse to a stop and, half-turning in the saddle, looked back, just in time to see Wedge-tail drop from the skies, down to the body of his late enemy. Evidently he had not completed his meal.

A little hysterically, the stockman said, "Peter, my lad, if we sneak back, you might get a chance to shoot old Wedge-tail with your airgun."

"Uncle Bert," replied the little boy in gravely-reproachful tones, "that good old eagle is my friend. I am not going to shoot him ever."

"It was only my stupid joke, Peter," said Summers, and then, in soft tones, "Wedge-tail, old boy, I take off my hat to you."

As the man and boy watched, they saw the eagle rise again, very slowly, and soar away into the heavens. They continued their silent vigil until the bird became a mere speck against the western sky, and then rode silently homewards.

They arrived just in time to find the two Flying Doctors ready to leave.

Little Peter had a deeply interesting story to tell and when he related how the eagle had dropped from the clouds in the very nick of time, and undoubtedly had saved him, if not from death, certainly from very serious injury, the listeners were deeply moved.

"And to think that I had murder in my heart towards that bird," said Dr. Grahame. "No matter what he has done, he has more than made up for it."

"Let me say 'amen' to that," echoed Gardiner.

"I always knew old Wedge-tail was a bird without compare," said Summers fervently. "If the rest of the birds around these parts ever want to elect a king, he is the one they have got to place the crown on!"

"I'm going straight inside to tell my dad he must not kill

any more eagles," said young Peter. "That old dog would have bitten me if Wedge-tail had not come along and killed it."

"Not the slightest doubt about that, my boy," said Summers, a lump in his throat as he recalled the grave peril in which the lad had been.

Shortly afterwards, the two Flying Doctors took off and were soon heading towards their distant base. Dr. Grahame led the way, and as he neared Wedge-tail's eyrie, he climbed high. Then, followed by Dr. Mason, he circled the lone peak once, paying a tribute to the great bird.

Perched in his lookout, Wedge-tail watched the two aeroplanes with angry concern, and if either or both had attempted to land in his tree, or even on the ground nearby, he would have attacked without counting the possible consequences. He watched them until they disappeared into the distant haze and then, fluffing out his feathers, prepared to doze. Taking everything into consideration, his day had been well spent, he considered. Of major importance was the fact that he had beaten a human being, even though it was a small one, in a contest for the possession of a half-bred dingo.

And so his days and weeks passed...

It was six months later that Jack Howard and Bert Summers, riding the paddocks in the first days of the lambing season, gazed at the sky and saw what ardently they had longed for.

"He's back again, bless his old heart!" said Howard softly. "I was half-afraid that when he left his eyrie months ago he'd never return." He grinned slyly. "Now then, Bert, go on, ask me how I know it is Wedge-tail!"

Bert Summers laughed happily.

"It's Wedge-tail all right," he began, and then broke off.

"Just a moment, Jack," he exclaimed. "What is that sailing up?"

Following his gaze, Howard noticed another eagle. It joined Wedge-tail and began to circle just below him.

"Looks very much as if old Wedge-tail has got married again," he said. "Well, good luck to the old chap. May he live long and die happy."

"That's all right, Jack, but it will mean more eagles to kill our sheep," said Summers, grinning. "All wedge-tails are lamb-killers, you know!"

"Now, don't rub it in, Bert," begged his friend. "I repeat, good luck to both of them. Wedge-tail's friends are my friends."

"Amen to that," said Summers softly.

As the two men sat loosely in their saddles watching them, the eagles, as if by some pre-arranged signal, ceased circling and began to glide off unhurriedly in the direction of a solitary mountain peak that towered into the distant sky like the upraised finger of a reclining giant. Smaller and smaller they became, until they were lost to human sight.

And with their vanishing figures went the good wishes of two men, one of whom had been the sworn enemy of their kind. But in that man's heart now there was nothing but friendliness towards that great old bird who, though he was as fierce and relentless as the country over which he hunted, was as the Creator of Birds had fashioned him.

In the eyes of these two men, he was justly entitled to the proud name they had bestowed upon him; Wedge tail, Monarch of the Western Skies.

THE END.

www.ingramcontent.com/pod-product-compliance
Lightning Source LLC
Chambersburg PA
CBHW072150020426
42334CB00018B/1938